W9-ARR-621

HOW TO TASTE

BECKY SELENGUT

HOW

TO

TA

The Curious Cook's Handbook to
Seasoning and Balance, from Umami
to Acid and Beyond—with Recipes

STE

SASQUATCH BOOKS
SEATTLE

Printed in China

Published by Sasquatch Books

22 21 20 19 18   9 8 7 6 5 4 3 2 1

Editor: Susan Roxborough
Production editor: Em Gale
Design and illustrations: Tony Ong
Copyeditor: Rachelle Longé McGhee

Library of Congress Cataloging-in-Publication Data is available.

Names: Selengut, Becky, author.
Title: How to taste : the curious cook's handbook to seasoning and balance,
    from umami to acid and beyond—with recipes / Becky Selengut.
Description: Seattle, WA : Sasquatch Books, [2018] | Includes bibliographical
    references and index.
Identifiers: LCCN 2017041100 | ISBN 9781632171054 (hardcover : alk. paper)
Subjects: LCSH: Cooking, American. | Flavor. | Cooking (Spices) | LCGFT:
    Cookbooks.
Classification: LCC TX715 .S14575 2018 | DDC 641.5973—dc23
LC record available at https://lccn.loc.gov/2017041100

ISBN: 978-1-63217-105-4

Sasquatch Books
1904 Third Avenue, Suite 710
Seattle, WA 98101
(206) 467-4300
www.sasquatchbooks.com

For April—I should have never doubted
you were a supertaster

Foreword XI   Introduction XIII

Chapter One   Chapter Eight
PRINCIPLES   # AROMATICS 111
OF TASTE 1   Chapter Nine
Chapter Two   # BITE 137
SALT 15   Chapter Ten
Chapter Three   # TEXTURE 171
ACID 37   Chapter Eleven
Chapter Four   # COLOR,
SWEET 51   # BOOZE,
Chapter Five   # AND
FAT 67   # EVERYTHING
Chapter Six   # ELSE 187
BITTER 83   Chapter Twelve
Chapter Seven   # THE TOTAL
UMAMI 95   # DISH 197

Acknowledgments 209   Bibliography 216
Appendix 210   Resources 217
Notes 211   Index 219

Recipe List

Spiced Carrot Salad 29

Ode to Gummy's Matzo
   Ball Soup 32

Italian Salsa Verde 45

Salmon with Miso Vinaigrette
   and Sesame-Roasted
   Vegetables 47

Honey, Rhubarb, and
   Thyme Jam 64

Cacao Nib and Chocolate
   Chunk Cookies 65

Roasted Winter Vegetables
   with Dates and Prosciutto
   Vinaigrette 76

Gummy's Brisket 78

Classic Manhattan 89

Warm Radicchio Salad with
   White Beans and Smoked
   Sea Salt 90

Coffee and Chocolate–Braised
   Short Ribs 91

Sweet Potato Soup with Chile
   and Lemongrass 105

Pasta alla Speranza 107

Dashi 108

Sri Lankan Spiced Rack of
   Lamb with Coconut Milk
   Sauce 133

Pickled Mangoes 135

Nuoc Cham 165

Fiery Roasted Thai Chile
   Chicken Wings 167

The Pantry's Southern-Style
   Hot Sauce 169

Texturally Superior BLAT 182

Tomato Salad with Mustard
   Caviar and Tomato-
   Cucumber Ice 184

Cinnamon and Ginger–
   Scented Lamb Stew with
   Tamarind Sauce and Saffron
   and Turmeric Rice Pilaf 205

FOREWORD

Follow a good recipe and you can be a good cook. Purchase the right ingredients, measure, chop, slice, grind, assemble, heat, assess doneness, and in the end the steps will probably create a dish that is close to what the recipe writer intended.

But to be a great cook? Great cooks don't just follow recipes; they understand flavors and how to balance them. They know that if the corn in the soup is super sweet, a squeeze of lime will keep it from cloying. If the eggplant in the baba ghanoush is bitter, they know a little more salt will mitigate it. They'll bump up the dill if the fricassee needs a lift and grate Grana into the potatoes if they need more savor. Great cooks know how to taste.

Becky is one of those great cooks. I hired her in 2001 when I was chef of the Herbfarm, which was something of a temple to Northwest seasonal ingredients and culinary herbs. She was intuitive, thoughtful, and wisecracking, and I loved working with her. Since those days, she has become an accomplished chef whose dishes pop with bright flavors. But Becky is also a great communicator and has expressed her passion for cooking through a career of writing and teaching.

When Becky first told me about her idea for this book I thought it was brilliant. So much is written on food and cooking—millions of recipes, volumes on cooking techniques, plenty on food science, but scarcely anything out there on what I would call flavor "theory." Her book explains how to identify flavors, how to build flavors, how to balance flavors, and how to fix a dish with flavors that go off balance. No easy task, but through her years of teaching cooking classes she can speak a language about flavor that inspires her students to be better cooks.

Becky has accomplished all that she set out to do. In this book, she codifies the elements of flavor, from sweet to bitter to fatty to umami to aromatic, and explains with clarity, insight, and wit how they work in a dish. Even though I've been rattling the pots and pans for four decades, reading this book has made me think about flavors in new ways and will undoubtedly make me a better cook too.

—**Jerry Traunfeld**, James Beard award–winning chef/ owner of Poppy and Lionhead restaurants in Seattle, Washington, and author of *The Herbfarm Cookbook* and *The Herbal Kitchen*

INTRODUCTION

"Season to taste" is the recipe writer's most colossal cop-out. Your recipe doesn't taste great? Well you must not have seasoned it properly! After all, we recipe writers are realists and we know that most home cooks adjust the ingredients and method, depending on what they have on hand and their own sense of creativity or inertia. "Season to taste" is vague enough to patch over a wealth of problems. Once the recipe leaves the writer's hands, different brands of stock, natural salt differences in produce, ingredient substitutions, and improper measurements can swing the pendulum of the recipe way off balance. For example, if you decide to scrap the capers I call for because you happen to think they're vile green orbs, that recipe just lost a lot of its salt, not to mention some acid and umami. That missing salt means the dish is no longer in the zone of proper seasoning.

Seasoning goes beyond salt, and if you're stymied by "season to taste" you might really be stuck once you think you've added enough salt and the dish still doesn't taste right. Most people know if their food is good or bad, but few know precisely why. If you've ever made a disaster of a dinner, been mystified by what the term "to taste" means, and had no bloody idea what went sideways, this book is for you.

My wife, April, has a specialty in the kitchen called "Oh SHIT!" because that's what I hear bouncing off the walls and up the stairwell each time she attempts to cook. This book is for her, but it's also for you. Even if her specialty is not yours and most of the time you get things to taste pretty good, this book will help you understand both your successes and failures and tip the balance toward the former.

I've been teaching students how to taste and season their food for much of my twenty-year career. I've noticed that when my students are unsure about what's wrong with the dish they can describe the problem while remaining unaware that their own words and body language signal the solution. Other times, when prompted, they use adjectives and gestures that are remarkably consistent from person to person. When a dish needs salt, they say "the flavor just falls off," "the carrot soup doesn't really taste carrot-y," "it seems like I taste it at first and then [making a downward gesture with their hand] there is nothing." If their shoulders shrug when they are talking, or if they say simply, "meh," well, it's definitely a salt problem. And yet I see so many people throw the whole kitchen sink at a salt problem, thinking that surely a handful of oregano and smoked paprika are the fix.

If a dish needs acidity (think vinegar or citrus), my students hang their hands down by their waist and say things about it like: "seems flat," "tastes really earthy," "seems lifeless and too heavy," or "it isn't vibrant, kind of dull." All of this points to a lack of proper acidity, or sourness. They implicitly know what is wrong with the food but don't have the decoder ring to unlock their own observations.

I'm not a professional baker, so this book will only touch on possible problems you might encounter with baking, though I provide references for great books on tweaking and understanding the science behind baking (see the Bibliography, page 216, for a few of my favorites). I'm also not a health professional, so this book is not meant to serve as a guide on which ingredients are better or worse for your health, though I may jump in with a word about certain things from time to time because I seriously can't help myself.

Telling you to "season to taste" does nothing to teach you *how* to taste—and that is precisely the lofty goal of this book. Once you know the most common culprits when your dish is out of whack, you'll save tons of time spinning your wheels grabbing for random solutions. You'll start thinking like a chef. Some people are born knowing how to do this—they are few and far between and most likely have more Michelin stars than you or I; the rest of us need to be taught. I've got your back.

HOW TO USE THIS BOOK

While it is certainly possible to skip around from one chapter to the next, I suggest that you start at the beginning, as I intend to build upon the concepts one puzzle piece at a time. At the very least, make sure you read all about the principles of taste in Chapter 1 before you proceed with the rest of the book. Why? Because literally nothing in this book, or in the rest of your life, will make any sense if you don't. Is that hyperbole? You bet it is, but still, read that first chapter.

Once you have that foundation, the rest of the chapters contain a few repeated elements that will reinforce the central concepts. **Recipes** will highlight the central lesson upon which each chapter is focused. **Experiment Time** is a feature intended to help you develop your palate. In these guided experiments I will be virtually testing and cooking alongside you, asking you to ponder certain questions and jot them down in a notebook. Then you can cheat and read the answers. **Cartoon Becky** will peek around the page occasionally to highlight an important lesson or point out nerdy things. Spoiler alert: Cartoon me is way cooler than actual me. Finally, **Fun Facts** will pop up here and there with cool tidbits I've discovered about the world of taste and flavor.

Chapter One

PRINCIPLES OF TASTE

How you taste a dish depends on many factors, among them your age; your genetics; your background and culture (if you were raised on lutefisk you just don't get why everyone else is disgusted by it); the medications you take; whether you're a smoker; whether you eat at restaurants frequently (greater salt tolerance); whether you frequently eat processed food (much greater salt tolerance); and most certainly many additional factors this relatively young science doesn't yet understand but will—sooner than later. The world of taste is subjective. What one person experiences when they taste a dish is not necessarily the same as someone else. Which means that no one can contest what it is that you, yourself, are tasting.

Despite this individuality in experience, there remains a common language among chefs about what dishes need and how to make them better. This shared lexicon exists in a diverse tasting world where science has identified the existence of *super-tasters*, which are those people with a greater density of taste buds and, arguably, more sensitivity in their palate; they make up about 25 percent of the population. Barb Stuckey, the author of the fantastic book *Taste What You're Missing*, refers to them as *sensitive tasters*; I agree with her, as there is nothing super about being over-whelmed by what you are tasting (such as catching many of the imperfections that can exist in wine). My wife, April, is trained as a sommelier and is also a super/sensitive taster. When I give her a piece of mango, she nearly gags: "This tastes like GRAVE DIRT." You might be wondering how anyone would know what grave dirt tastes like (best not to ask), but you get my point: there's nothing so super about being a supertaster. Most of us—approximately 50 percent of the population—are *average tasters* and the other 25 percent are considered *tolerant tasters* (those with the lowest density of taste buds). Despite these physical differences in taste sensitivity and tongue composition, everyone can learn how to taste more astutely and, in so doing, learn how to make their food taste better to them.

TASTER STATUS: CHEFS VERSUS SOMMELIERS

When I tested chef friends with a PROP strip (more about this on page 8), I found that all of them were average tasters—picky super/sensitive tasters most likely wouldn't be interested in pursuing a career in food—while word on the street is that many wine experts are super/sensitive tasters, easily able to pick out imbalances in wine and choose extremely well-made ones for their clients. I only tested two sommeliers: my wife, a sensitive taster, and my friend Chris, who tested as average.

Much like wine experts learn how to identify the subtle nuances in the glass (nuances that sound to the rest of us like "I'm getting asparagus on the nose, lead and gooseberries on the palate," even if that's not at all what they said), home cooks can also learn to pull out taste and flavor notes by focus, repetition, and experimentation. Most of us will never breathe in such rarefied air to pull out an obscure spice in a blind sniff test (I struggled to name coriander when it was waved under my nose during a late-night challenge in my house), and yet I firmly believe anyone can go from food rube to rock star with focus and effort. That being said, it's a neat party trick if you can nail the spice on the first try.

We're talking about food in this book, but fine-tuning your conscious sensory appreciation can enrich many areas of your life. Years ago, while walking in the woods, I recall being able to identify maybe one or two trees here, a smattering of plants there. I appreciated the woods, for certain, and would stop to pick a huckleberry or smell a wildflower, but I also walked through them thinking of my to-do list, lost in my mind. My friend Susan, a forest ecologist, took me on a hike one early spring day and by the time we had walked a quarter mile, she had taught me at least five new trees and twenty new plants. She had me crush the leaf of an Indian plum tree and hold it up to my nose. She smiled knowingly when the aroma hit the olfactory cells at the back of my nose, sending a very clear message from my brain to my mouth: "Cucumber!" I said, a little too loud. The next time I went for a walk in the woods the forest leaped out at me, alive in a way I had never experienced before. My focus snapped to the present; I was all in. In psychology, they call it "flow" or being "in the zone." It's when you're immersed fully in the activity, energized and capable of intense, surprising focus. My walks in the woods were never quite the same.

When you start tasting food as eagerly and intentionally as most chefs do, you will notice a deepened sensory connection to the food that—not to be too Buddhist about it—connects you to the moment, taking a bit of the chore out of cooking and adding a layer of peaceful contemplation as an unintended but welcome side dish.

But in order to reach Contemplative Food Buddha, you must first start with the basics. In the next six chapters we'll get into what scientists refer to as the *basic tastes*: salt, acid, sweet, fat, bitter, and umami.[1, 2] Tastes, as distinguished from flavors, originate in the taste buds of the tongue and mouth (and the rest of the body). In the following three chapters we'll cover aromatics (herbs and spices), bite (chiles, peppercorns), and texture (crunch, astringency). The last two chapters cover some bonus material: color, booze, temperature, sound, and the company you keep. In total, these twelve chapters represent what I have found are the most important elements of a dish. To arrive at these elements, I studied the current research on taste and flavor but ultimately I leaned more heavily on my own process for creating a balanced, satisfying dish. When I eat a magnificent dish, I sometimes reverse engineer it according to the ten elements identified in this book, and nearly every time, the majority are in play and kept in perfect balance.

Great dishes consider most—if not all—of these elements, and poor dishes usually fail to.

> **FUN FACT** Did you know that your gut has a refined palate? Taste receptors—or perhaps more accurately, *chemical* receptors—for the basic tastes exist in our guts and lungs, and gentlemen, wow, here's your trivia fact of the century: in your testicles.

Technically "flavor" refers to what we perceive as basic tastes plus texture, pain reception, and aroma. In fact, many scientists theorize that much of a food's flavor has to do with the olfactory system rather than simply what we perceive through our taste receptors. No studies have definitively confirmed this, but anecdotally, it truly seems that food is less interesting when your nose is stuffed up.

If you'd had a seat at the table one frigid winter afternoon when my siblings and I made my grandmother laugh so hard her nose turned into a hot chocolate dispenser, you'd agree that it's probably best that we have a redundant system when it comes to issues of breathing and eating. As a six-year-old, having no reason to believe that the nose and the mouth were internally connected, I thought my grandmother had performed the most miraculous of magic tricks. It goes in her mouth and comes out her nose. How did she do it?

I learned later that this redundancy is precisely where things get interesting. As we pass that cup of hot chocolate under our nose and breathe in, volatile aromas are released and directed toward olfactory receptor cells through our nasal passages (orthonasal olfaction) that send a message (electrical signals) to our brain. The messages get sent to our brain's olfactory bulb, which is directly connected to the amygdala and hippocampus, two areas where emotion and memory live. So if you've smelled hot chocolate before, the connection is made, the brain engages the language center, and within a blink of an eye, if you're me, you say, "Ah . . . this hot chocolate smells just like the one my grandmother shot out of her nose that day . . ." If we're still interested in drinking the hot chocolate, we lift the mug to our mouth, take a sip, and volatile aromas head toward the back of the mouth and then up into the nasal passage where they hit those same olfactory cells (retronasal olfaction). Therefore, we "smell" food in our mouth, not just in our nose. Some might argue that we smell better retronasally since we've broken down the food and warmed it up while chewing, potentially releasing more aromatics.

> **FUN FACT** A recent study published in *Science* magazine suggests that humans can discriminate more than one trillion olfactory stimuli.[3] Scientists now believe that our sense of smell may outperform our eyes and ears. Put more simply, truffle pigs: watch your backs—turns out humans can smell way better than we previously thought and we are theoretically less likely to eat the truffles without a bowl of pasta in hand. We are coming for your job.

Smell and taste are linked together in a fascinating dance of perception, recognition, memory, and emotional connection. But at the end of the day, smell, whether it comes from inside the mouth or through the nose, is a significant driver of flavor and perception of pleasure. One person's reaction upon catching a whiff of *natto* (fermented soybeans often eaten with rice for breakfast in Japan), for example, might be pure joy, but for those not raised on it, it reeks of sweaty feet, blue cheese, and death.

Aroma is such a huge part of the flavor picture that loss of smell (anosmia) might be a worse fate for a chef than loss of a hand.

Let's break this smell and taste thing down a bit: If I were to give you a coconut-flavored jelly bean and ask you to describe it, you'd probably say it was "sweet" and perhaps correctly identify it as "coconut" (if you've had coconut before and can call up the memory). Sweet is the basic taste sent to the brain via sweet receptors located in the taste buds, whereas coconut is the flavor gathered largely from what your olfactory cells told your brain it recognized—combined, less so, with what you tasted. Despite the fact that scientists view taste and flavor as distinctly different, I tend to use the words somewhat interchangeably because I'm a chef, not a food scientist, and cooking, like language, can sometimes be imperfect. If you pinched your nose and held your breath and tried that jelly bean again, you'd likely identify that it was sweet and chewy and not have much else to say. Unblock your nose as you continue to chew, breathe in and out through your nose to engage both ortho- and retronasal olfaction, and suddenly there it is: coconut.

TASTE VERSUS FLAVOR

The six basic tastes (salt, acid, sweet, fat, bitter, and umami) are figured out in the mouth (along with temperature, the "heat" of chiles or the "cooling" of mint, and texture—including astringency), but flavor, as a concept, combines these basic tastes and qualities along with aroma and memory to lead your brain to come up with a complete picture.

Taste Receptors

Remember when you learned that you taste sweet at the tip of your tongue and bitter at the back, salt and sour at the sides? You do? Great, now totally forget that idea, along with the tongue map that every elementary school teacher in the '60s, '70s, and '80s (and possibly into the '90s) used; it turns out it was a gross oversimplification of an experiment done in 1901 by German scientist David P. Hänig. Touch a lemon wedge to the tip of your tongue and you will quickly appreciate its sourness. Exclusive zones of taste sensation might have made for an easy-to-digest infographic, but the truth is that you can detect these tastes all over your tongue, though it is true that you have more sweet receptors at the tip, more bitter receptors at the back, and fewer taste buds overall in the middle of your tongue (what I will refer to as the mid-palate).[4] This will be especially important when determining if you've added enough salt to a dish (see Chapter 2).

Here's a simplified explanation of what is happening on your tongue when you eat a bite of food: Small bumps on the tongue (fungiform papillae) house taste buds. Each bud has around 50 to 150 taste receptor cells on it. As you eat, protein receptors bind to small molecules communicating the presence of sweet, bitter, umami, and possibly fat; in the case of salt and acid, it's suggested that signals are activated through ion channels. Most people have about ten thousand taste buds at their disposal, which regenerate every ten days or so. As a person ages, some of these taste buds peace out and don't go back to work. In fact, this starts to happen around the age of 40, which means that you might require more salt on your food and formerly flavorful foods may progressively lose their punch. You can mitigate the extent of this loss by not smoking; smoking hinders the ability to taste. All is not hopeless, though, my middle-aged and older friends, at least in the case of smell: a study on perfumers found that the olfactory parts of their brains grew more developed as they aged.[5] Directing extra focus toward what you are smelling, in the school of "use it or lose it," might increase your abilities as you age.

Taster Types

Experimental psychologist Linda Bartoshuk and her colleagues coined the term "supertaster" at Yale University in the early '90s after doing experiments on numbers of taste buds and volunteers' ability to detect the bitterness of a certain chemical (6-n-propylthiouracil, or PROP) in thyroid medications. Being a super/sensitive taster is genetically inherited. Tasters of this type are more sensitive eaters, finding food to be fairly overwhelming at times. Keep in mind that science still has much to uncover in the world of taste and flavor, so while you might not personally react to PROP, putting you in the tolerant or average taster camps, there are twenty to thirty bitter-receptor families. You might not have the gene to detect PROP, but you might detect the other families just fine—there simply isn't a scientific test to determine as much yet.

Use the following methods as a general guide for determining taster type but not as an end statement on how you taste. There is still so much we don't know about taste sensitivity in humans.

Method #1

Purchase PROP test strips (see page 217 for source information). They are easily available online and inexpensive. You put the test strip in your mouth, move it around, and if it tastes like nothing, you are considered a tolerant taster; if it's very mildly bitter, you are considered an average taster; if it's horribly bitter, you are considered a super/sensitive taster. Be sure to spit it out.

Method #2

Grab some blue food coloring and a paper-hole reinforcement (the little donut stickers that kept paper from ripping out of your Trapper Keeper. Remember those?). Then grab a friend and do as follows:

1 Have your friend add one drop of blue food coloring to the tip of your tongue.

2 Swish some water around in your mouth and then spit it out.

3 Swallow a few times to dry your mouth. The blue dye will have colored your tongue blue but left the fungiform papillae (where your taste receptors are) lighter in color (whitish or pinkish).

4 Have your friend place a paper-hole reinforcement on the tip of your tongue.

5 Have your friend take a photo of the area within the hole. Make sure it's in focus!

6 Blow up the photo and count how many obvious large taste buds you can see. Ignore the very tiny ones. Generally speaking, if you have thirty or more taste buds, you are probably a super/sensitive taster; fifteen to thirty indicates an average taster and fewer than fifteen a tolerant taster.

7 Beg your friend to delete the photo of your Smurfy tongue to prevent them from posting it on social media with a quip about how you lack taste.

If you're alone, use a mirror to help you get the blue dye on your tongue and place the paper-hole reinforcement. Finally, take 50 of the world's most bizarre selfies (one of them will be in focus).

FUN FACT In a study of 4,000 Americans, Linda Bartoshuk, internationally known researcher specializing in the chemical senses of taste and smell, found that 34 percent of the study population of supertasters were women while only 22 percent were men.[6]

Method #3

This way is completely anecdotal and unscientific, but it's worth asking yourself these questions and considering where you may fall on the spectrum.

1   Are you pretty happy with your food and don't understand why everyone around you is so picky? If anything, do you find food to be fairly bland? Do you love adding extra salt to everything, along with hot sauce? Do you tolerate grapefruit juice, brussels sprouts, and radicchio? You're probably a tolerant taster. There's an increased likelihood if you enjoy extra-hoppy bitter beers or if you've been drinking black coffee since the age of eight.

2   Do you have a handful of foods you don't love but you are generally easy to please? Do you like brussels sprouts, radicchio, and endive if they are cooked or seasoned in such a way as to cut their bitterness? When you follow recipes at home or eat out, are you generally satisfied and feel that more often than not the food is balanced and seasoned well? Did you start drinking coffee with cream and sugar and then learned to tolerate it with less cream and sugar (or eventually none at all)? You're most likely an average taster.

3   Do you dislike most vegetables but tolerate the sweeter ones (corn, peas, carrots)? Do you find coffee, olives, dark chocolate, and hoppy beers intolerable? Do people in your life constantly tell you how picky you are? Do you stick to the same foods all the time and are generally unadventurous about trying new dishes? Are you sensitive to chiles and prefer things not too spicy? Do you find yourself often adding more salt to your food at the table? (To find out why you might do that, read Chapter 6.) You are most likely a super/sensitive taster. Sorry, food is sometimes an overwhelming experience for you—even the slightest imbalances in dishes or foods are difficult for you to tolerate. Take comfort: it's not your fault (though exposing yourself to disliked foods can move you toward greater tolerance, if not eventually love).

Tasting Tips

I'm sure you've seen or heard wine experts swishing, slurping, and sucking in their cheeks while tasting wine. Have you ever wondered why we don't teach chefs and cooks to do the same with food (aside from aspiration fears)? Turns out there is much to be learned from the world of wine and here I've applied some of those tasting tips to food.

- While not entirely attractive, pushing food from the top of your tongue up to the roof of your mouth while breathing out activates the retronasal receptors, making it easier for you to get the most out of tasting.

- Try closing your eyes next time you taste something. Shutting down one sense (sight) to focus on another (taste) is often very helpful in getting you to pinpoint what is missing in food.

- Make sure to let salt or other ingredients (acid, fat, aromatics) mix completely into food before tasting it, otherwise you might get a false read on what the dish needs. This is most important when adding salt or something like cayenne pepper.

- Most people murmur "mmm" after tasting something they like. In paying close attention to my own reactions when I taste, I realized that when the dish is good but not quite perfectly balanced, I utter a short "mm," but my brows are furrowed and there is a question mark. If you notice yourself doing this, seize the moment! Now is the time to take a small amount of the food from the bigger dish and (using what you learn in this book) test your theory to make the dish even better—add a little more salt or acid or aromatics or whatever you think it needs, but I bet it's salt. Did the addition make it more delicious? Is that "mm" now an "mmmmm"? Did you just high-five yourself? Yes? That was it. Adjust the larger batch and STOP. Or perhaps the addition made your brows furrow more? No more "mmm"-ing at all? Whoops. That wasn't it. Take out another sample and try again. Don't test more than one theory at a time.

- Not only can you burn yourself sampling really hot food, the heat tends to dull your perception of flavor. Wait until it cools off a bit to get a better read on what you are tasting.
- Perfectly seasoned food will be muted when you try it cold out of the refrigerator the next day. Always taste leftovers at the temperature you plan on serving them. If you taste them at a different temperature you won't get an accurate read on the flavor. If you end up changing the serving temperature, you may need to adjust the seasoning.

Taste Is Subjective

Taste is as subjective as music or art. One person's disdain for the bands Anthrax or Pussy Riot could be another's jam. One person's jam might literally be jam; someone else might hate it. They are both right. This is why we often say there's no accounting for taste (though, c'mon Pussy Riot haters, they're pretty awesome). Despite this subjectivity, an understanding of the basic principles that underpin music, art, or food enriches your appreciation. Even with these basic principles in mind, creators at the top of their game often twist or break the rules of their discipline, and it is sometimes in the twisting that true genius emerges. However, even the geniuses most likely first learned the core principles of their discipline. Start by understanding the basics, and then get in the kitchen and break all the rules.

And speaking of subjectivity, if you have ever wondered if you're just "tasting it all wrong" or if you've been accused of not having a very "good" palate, you never need to defend your personal perceptions. Rely most heavily on what you—and you alone—are experiencing. No book, scientist, or peer pressure from a friend can make you like something you simply don't like.

That being said, you should really try natto, just so you can appreciate how foul it is. Sorry, Japan! I love you in a million other ways.

Many people can make a good dish; this book will help you make good food truly great. Let's do this.

TOP 5 SIGNS A COOKBOOK ISN'T WORTH YOUR CASH

1   If you read a few recipes and notice they don't mention anything about the type of salt recommended, or if the addition of salt isn't mentioned until the very end of the recipes, be skeptical. See Chapter 2 for an explanation of why, for most dishes, you should salt early and often, and how the volume of salt will vary widely depending on what kind you use.

2   If the book tells you to make a vinaigrette based on a 3:1 oil-to-acid ratio. See Chapter 3 for why that's typically inaccurate.

3   If a book uses the word *umami* to describe something that has no protein in it. See Chapter 7 for an explanation of how protein is required for something to have umami.

4   If you are advised to use only ground spices and to add those spices directly to a water-based soup (no toasting, no infusion in oil or fat), or if the book has recipes calling for fresh herbs in why-bother amounts of 1 teaspoon. Read Chapter 8 to understand the importance of aromatics.

5   Head to the index and look for *caramelized onions*. If there is an entry, head to the page and read the method. If it says it will take fewer than 10 minutes, they are delusional and the entire cookbook can't be trusted. Read more about why in Chapter 9. (And watch my video on how to caramelize onions correctly here: bit.ly/2pytOrx.)

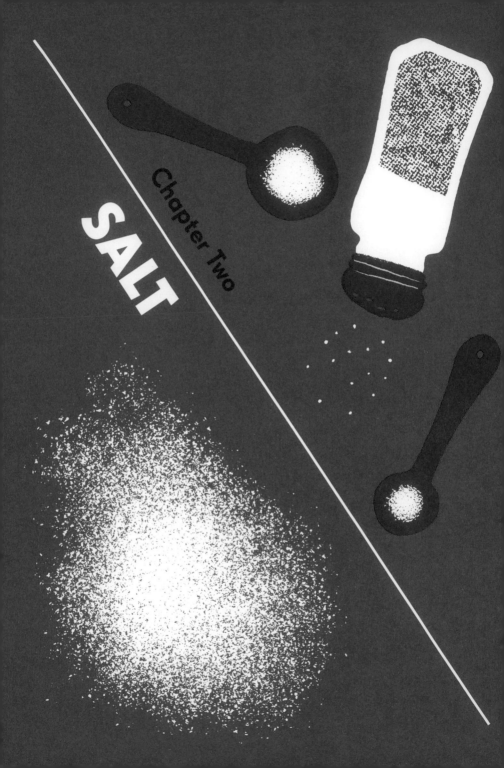

Chapter Two

SALT

First-year culinary students stand out for many reasons, not the least of which is the dorky white paper hat. I can spot a first-year student's recipe from a mile away. I know. I was there. I made all the same mistakes.

What stands out most is their desire to leap far beyond the knowledge they have—to throw everything at the wall, all at the same time, like a child excited by shiny new toys. A first-year culinary student will squirt marjoram oil on a plate, dribble on dots of beet puree, add a powder of toasted brioche, arrange a piece of salmon and raw razor clams, finish it all with a fish sauce emulsion and snail foam, and then stand back and look around for affirmation that they are only in school for the credits, for they could be winning *Top Chef* right this minute. I jest, but only a little.

The problem with all this enthusiasm is that the cart is miles before the horse. A taste of that beet puree reveals that it is woefully underseasoned, and when I say "seasoned" I mean salted (see my rant on page 164). The razor clams, on the other hand, have so much added salt that they are moving across the plate looking for the ocean. In an attempt to create complexity, the entire dish is uneven, overdone, inconsistent. Some ingredients have no right to share real estate with some of the others. But the most important take home here—and the hardest one to learn—is that salt is almost always the problem and almost always the solution.

Putting aside using high-quality, seasonal ingredients, salt is the first and last thing in creating excellent dishes. Everything else, whether it be herbs, spices, or chiles, is a bonus. Salt is the volume knob on your stereo, turning up the essence of your ingredients, bringing into focus the complexity of all that goes into a carrot or a steak or a piece of bread. A properly salted dish won't be salty. It will taste more of itself. A carrot soup will taste more carroty: sweeter, more nuanced. Salt helps ingredients sing and, when done with a careful hand and a patient palate, makes all the difference in the world. Skip past mastering salt and all manner of gorgeous plating and potentially fascinating flavor combinations will fall hideously flat.

But snail foam? That can never be made good.

Salt 101

Salt is what's known as a *flavorant*; it doesn't contribute a flavor all on its own but brings out the flavor of other ingredients (sugar and MSG are other examples of flavorants). Salt is a significant component of what makes our bodies tick, driving nerve and muscle function and regulating cellular water balance. A serious salt deficiency can lead to death. Most Americans have the opposite problem. Too much sodium in the diet has been linked to high blood pressure and other cardiovascular problems. But before you remove salt from your kitchen, keep in mind that the vast majority of salt (over 75 percent) in the American diet comes from processed foods and restaurant dishes.[7] Salting to maximize flavor in home-cooked meals such that the food is palatable without tasting salty is not the main culprit here.

My experience is that pleasing home-cooked food is more likely to satisfy you and curb cravings. Michael Moss, author of *Salt Sugar Fat*, an exposé on the processed food industry, notes "how aggressive the industry [is] wielding not only salt, but sugar and fat too. These are the pillars of processed foods, the three ingredients without which there would be no processed foods. Salt, sugar, and fat drive consumption by adding flavor and allure. But surprisingly, they also mask bitter flavors that develop in the manufacturing process. They enable these foods to sit in warehouses or on the grocery shelf for months." The perception of salt can be altered by increasing the acidity and sweetness in processed foods. In other words, processed food manufacturers increase the levels of salt, sugar, and fat to create an irresistible and, many would argue, addictive profile. You at home, on the other hand, are most likely not engineering your dishes to get your family addicted to salt, sugar, and fat. In your home kitchen you are unlikely to play the same games with your food. From what I've seen, most home cooks are actually scared of using salt and therefore woefully underseason their food.

Salt works synergistically with umami, that savory basic taste that makes meat, mushrooms, and aged cheeses irresistible. When salt and umami get together, they become more than the sum of their parts (see Chapter 7 for more on umami). Salt also helps strengthen gluten (the protein matrix that gives structure and elastic chew to breads and baked goods), so it's important to add it to pasta, bread, and pizza doughs—and not just for the flavor benefits.

Salt also helps to release food's tantalizing aromas. A simple experiment, suggested by *Saveur* editor Max Falkowitz, that demonstrates this involves smelling an onion as you cook it, before and after adding salt. You should notice that the smell is far more concentrated and tempting a few seconds after you add the salt. Likewise, the smell of a steak on a grill—not as amazing without the salt.

Most importantly: salting "early and often," as I tell my students, can make a huge difference in the end result. Adding salt to onions while they sauté, for example, can speed up the cooking process by encouraging the sweating out of liquids (via the process of osmosis). Say you are making a chunky potato soup. You neglect to salt the onions when starting the soup and forget to salt again when adding the potatoes and liquid. As the potatoes soften and swell, they expand with the liquid—that bland liquid. When you season the soup at the end, you find that no matter how much salt you add, the potatoes themselves fall flat. You end up oversalting the broth in an attempt to make up for the tasteless potatoes. What you are left with is an inconsistent soup, with parts simultaneously too salty and too bland. The only way to fix this soup is to puree it.

I learned from Judy Rodgers's *Zuni Cafe Cookbook* the power of salting meats early. Bigger cuts of meat (roasts, leg of lamb, large birds) require a longer pre-salting time. Thinner pieces, such as rib or loin chops, need much less time. I salt or dry-brine turkeys a few days ahead, individual steaks that morning. After 5 minutes or so, osmosis draws moisture out of the meat and combines with the salt, which is why the worst time to cook a steak is a few minutes up to 40 minutes after salting, as the surface moisture will just evaporate in the hot pan, leading to a dry steak. Wait, ideally, at least an hour after salting to cook your steak as the salt, now dissolved in the water released by the steak, will be absorbed back into the meat (reverse osmosis). With even more time (I refrigerate salted steaks for 6 to 8 hours), the salt penetrates the meat (diffusion), altering the protein structure and allowing it to absorb more liquid. If you forget to salt the meat ahead, salt it as you put it into the hot pan, before the moisture has a chance to bead up on the surface.[8]

> **FUN FACT** Pregnant women become less sensitive to salt, desiring more of it; scientists theorize that this decreased sensitivity encourages women to consume greater amounts at a time when extra fluids and nutrients would be helpful to the mother and fetus.[9]

Pre-salting beaten eggs and letting them sit for 10 minutes before cooking them makes a world of difference in how creamy they are as well. Note that the color darkens slightly in pre-salted eggs, but I find that the added creaminess is worth the subtle color change. (Check out my video for making perfect scrambled eggs here: bit.ly/2qGrr3F.) Even sturdy vegetables, such as onions and eggplant, can benefit from an early salting. But not everything should be salted ahead: Tender lettuce leaf salads will break down a bit and tomatoes will weep. Seafood, due to its delicate texture, won't hold up well (unless you're curing it), because the flesh can become leathery and chewy. However, a quick dip of a fish fillet in a wet brine or salting 30 minutes or less in advance can season the fish throughout, though I typically don't find it necessary.

One of salt's most impressive powers is its ability to suppress unpleasant bitterness in foods; it does this while also accentuating more desirable aspects, such as sweetness. If you add a pinch of salt to a grapefruit half, the salt rounds out the flavor, suppressing some of the bitterness and turning up the typically more muted, sweeter aspects of the fruit. I always add at least a pinch of salt to all my desserts to enhance the sweetness and bring forward the star flavors of the dish, no matter what kind of dessert it is. In certain desserts I add more than just a pinch of salt to really highlight the contrast between salty and sweet. Anyone who is as addicted to chocolate chip cookies with sea salt on top or salted caramel ice cream knows exactly what I mean.

Without salt, there is a lack of unity in a dish. A lack of balance. Certain ingredients taste too strong, others not enough, and the resulting composition may not mesh together well. Imagine a disorganized a cappella group: the tenor is a diva screaming his words, the alto is aggressively yelling back, the baritone is taking a smoke break, the bass is barely detectable, the first and second soprano are singing down the hall. What they need is a conductor—a leader to bring them together and run the show, coaxing out the best of each member and toning down any too dominant. Salt is the conductor for food, weaving ingredients together, allowing you to pick out certain notes, blending others, leaving you with one pleasingly complex and unified harmony.

How to Determine if Salt Is the Missing Ingredient

It's easier than you might think, though practice and focus are required. We have fewer taste buds in the middle part of our tongue (the mid-palate) than anywhere else. Use this knowledge to your advantage—the mid-palate is the place where taste sensations die off a bit, so bump up the salt incrementally until the transition from tongue tip to throat is a seamless one. When food is undersalted, you may have the sensation of a metaphorical hole opening up in the center of your tongue where the flavor falls off precipitously. You could sense the food's potential when it hit the tip of your tongue but then it travels backward and meh, there it went. Perhaps there's a brief sensation at the back of the tongue (especially with bitter flavors) before it disappears again. This is what a dish tastes like when it is woefully undersalted.

However, gradual additions of salt will start to bridge that mid-palate and allow the balanced taste to move farther and farther back on your tongue. When you have finally added enough salt, the flavor persists consistently from front to back and has a lingering finish much like good wines. Ideally all of this transpires without the food tasting salty at all—on the contrary, the flavor should be even, without one thing dominating another.

This is probably obvious, but while salt brings out the essential flavor of whatever ingredient or dish you apply it to, if you start with subpar components, the salt can only help so much. A properly seasoned salad made with last week's tired ingredients is just barely better than an unseasoned salad made with last week's tired ingredients.

DECIPHERING A SALT PROBLEM

When food is undersalted you may detect the following:

- The sensation of a piece of cotton or gauze wrapped around the middle of your tongue, dulling sensation
- A loss of taste as the food hits your mid-palate
- Tasting some elements of the dish but missing others
- A feeling that each element in the dish is fighting against another

How to Fix an Oversalted Dish

1 Bulk up or dilute: in other words, add more of the other ingredients to spread that salt around. If you made a salty salad, toss in more lettuce. Soup? Add cream or some (unsalted) stock to dilute it. What you shouldn't do? Add a cut-up potato to said soup to "suck out the extra salt." Seriously, don't. It doesn't work and you could end up introducing unwanted starchiness. Some kitchen myths just won't die.

2 Add some sweetness in the form of sugar, honey, dried fruit, etc. Your brain will be absolutely convinced there's less salt in the food. Surprise, there isn't.

3 Add lemon juice or vinegar in small amounts, toss or stir well, and keep tasting until you detect less saltiness. Acid turns down the perception of salt. If you often find restaurant food too salty, ask for a lemon wedge or some vinegar; you might still end up with cankles from water retention but you'll enjoy your meal more.

4 Add fat to "coat the tongue," which will lessen the perception of salt. For example, add some coconut milk to a salty Thai soup, or whisk a little extra olive oil into an oversalted dressing.

5 Try any combination of 1, 2, 3, and 4 if one on its own isn't doing the trick.

THE CURIOUS CASE OF THE SALTY TORTILLA CHIP

Scenario: I ask you to make a simple guacamole using an avocado, a pinch of salt, and a lime. You taste it and feel like there's not enough salt, but you theorize that when you eat it with the salty chips there will be plenty of salt to boost the flavor of the guacamole.

Question: When you dip the chip into the undersalted guacamole, will the salty tortilla chip boost its flavor? What is the lingering taste in your mouth: avocado or the corn in the tortilla chip?

Answer: When pairing a dip with a chip, you have to match the salt levels or the saltier of the two ends up dominating. In this case, the flavor of the corn in the tortilla chip will be what you predominantly taste. When pairing foods, always try each component with its intended accompaniment to see if the total experience is spot on. Add more salt to that guacamole—enough that it might be too salty to eat on its own but it will balance out that salty chip and elevate the flavor of the avocado to its proper place of prominence. The salt on that chip is doing its job very well: highlighting the essential taste of corn, to the exclusion of the taste of avocado when they are combined. It may seem counterintuitive to add more salt to a dip mixed with a salty chip, but it works. Try it.

Types of Salt

Have you ever tried iodized table salt, just on its own? If you use it regularly and haven't, I think you should, and then compare it to the flavor of kosher salt or fine sea salt and see which you prefer. One of the first things we did in culinary school was a blind tasting of various kinds of salt. I was shocked when I realized what I had written down in my notes: the iodized salt was sharp, had a chemical aftertaste, and was my least favorite. That had been the only salt in my life up until that moment.

But that experiment just highlights the subtle flavors of the salt (or more likely, the flavor of the added iodine); when it comes down to it, salt—in any form: iodized, kosher, fine or flaky sea salt—is salt is salt is salt. Which is to say that, generally speaking, it will do the same thing to bring out the flavors of your food, balance the various elements, and create chemical and physical changes through osmosis, brining, curing, et cetera.

I personally use kosher salt for large tasks, such as salting pasta water, blanching vegetables, or salt-encrusting fish, because it's cheaper and easy to pinch with your fingers. Diamond Crystal brand is my favorite for flavor and texture, and bonus, it doesn't contain an anticaking agent, which, in my opinion, is an unnecessary additive. I use fine sea salt for seasoning as I cook and almost everything else. Occasionally I use flaky or chunky sea salt for finishing a dish to get a little extra crunchy burst. Again, however, for the purposes of how salt affects the palatability of food, you can exchange one salt for another, though keep in mind that kosher and flaky salts take up more volume than fine sea or table salts. I recommend a 1:1.75 ratio of table salt to kosher salt for best results when converting a recipe.

SALT CONVERSIONS

For every 1 teaspoon table salt called for in a recipe, use 1¾ teaspoons Diamond Crystal kosher salt. Table salt and fine sea salt are 1:1 in quantities less than a tablespoon, but use slightly more fine sea salt than table salt when you get into larger quantities: 1 tablespoon table salt to 1 tablespoon plus ¼ teaspoon fine sea salt. Note: Morton's coarse kosher salt is much flatter and denser than Diamond Crystal and can be used 1:1 for table salt, but I still recommend Diamond over other brands.

When following the experiments in this book, in order to standardize expected results, please pay close attention to the type and amount of salt specified. I will ask you to use either fine sea salt or kosher salt.

If You Need to Cook with Less Salt

The US Department of Health's 2015 Dietary Guidelines for Americans advises that most Americans limit their daily sodium intake to less than 2,300 milligrams (approximately 1 teaspoon of table salt). If you regularly exceed this recommendation and would benefit from a salt-restricted diet, there are several things you can do when cooking at home to help yourself or your uncle Bob make the adjustment. Poor Uncle Bob.

1   Be patient—as you wean yourself from added salt, you will become more and more attuned to the natural saltiness of foods; eventually you will require less to perceive that a dish tastes good.

2   It is sometimes advised that one should compensate for less salt in the diet by increasing the use of herbs and spices (aromatics) to make food more interesting. Be careful when heeding this advice, though, as many herbs and spices have bitter undertones, and the tempering abilities of salt will not be in play, therefore highlighting the imbalance. For example, adding extra cumin, oregano, and thyme to a salt-less chili would add a level of bitterness that many would

find unpalatable. Instead reach for herbs and spices that are naturally less bitter to add interest and variety to that same dish: cilantro and sweet paprika, for example.

3   Make sure to choose fresh, colorful ingredients with varied textures, as this will help add greater interest to a dish.

4   That being said, resist the urge to use a ton of different ingredients in an effort to add complexity to low-salt dishes. Remember that salt is the conductor of the ingredient orchestra. Without salt, dishes may taste disjointed and unbalanced, and this will only become more exaggerated the more ingredients there are.

5   Reduce processed and packaged food in your diet to help reset your palate, effectively increasing your sensitivity to salt. You'll need less to be satisfied.

How I Learned to Make the World's Worst (Then Best) Matzo Ball Soup

Even though I learned about salt in the first week of culinary school, it was only a few months later that I found myself standing in my kitchen staring down at a bland pot of matzo ball soup completely dumbfounded by what could possibly be missing. The soup, it turns out, started with a pinch too much hubris. I was trying to re-create my grandmother's recipe, the liquid penicillin of my youth and the most comforting thing anyone in my family can think to do with a chicken. But being that I was on my way to becoming a chef, I decided I could certainly one-up Gummy. I would apply the solid French culinary technique I was learning at school to her soup—I would take something already wonderful and make it magnificent.

I sat down and scribbled some notes. First thing to go: Gummy's old-world technique of throwing the whole chicken into the pot to make the broth. (After all, by the time the stock was done, the white meat that would eventually be served in the soup bowl would be overdone.) Instead, I'd break down the bird, separate the dark meat from white meat, and cook the thighs first, adding the white meat later. I'd roast the bones along with some extra necks and backs for better body and caramelize them for a richer, deeper flavor. I'd deglaze the roasting pan with a little white wine and marry the flavorful liquid from the pan to the stock along with some thyme, bay, fennel, leeks, and carrots. After several hours and careful straining, I'd reduce the stock for greater flavor. Then I'd grab a new pot, add some chicken fat, and start anew with onion, fennel, carrot, leek, and celery. Gummy always cooked her matzo balls in water; I'd simmer mine in a mixture of water and stock so they could absorb extra flavor. At the very end, I'd combine the stock, the perfectly cooked meat, and the plump matzo balls.

The aroma was beguiling. I went in for a taste. It tasted more like nothing than nothing. Surely something was wrong with my palate. I tried again. Same result. All that time, all that effort, and it tasted like someone had waved a chicken over the top of a pot of tepid water. I'm being generous when I say this.

So what went wrong? In culinary school we were warned to never salt stocks, and for good reason. Stocks are the workhorses of most professional kitchens and they are used in numerous ways. A cook can never know all the eventual uses for a stock, and if it gets reduced down a lot, as in a demi-glace, the addition of salt to the stock could ultimately lead to a nearly inedible end product. So, salt early and often—except with stock. However, once you have progressed to using your stock in a soup, where you reduce only minimally, it's time to pull out that maxim again and start salting. I had been so focused on not salting my stock that when it came to building the flavor in my soup, well, I forgot. I did remember to salt the matzo balls, but my first taste was of the broth alone.

Man, did I have such high expectations. The smell in the house was ridiculously good, my cockiness and self-satisfaction at an all-time high. And that bland dishwater masquerading as soup was so very humbling. Being fairly new to cooking, I believed I had ruined the dish—that all that time, all that focus, all those extra steps led to nothing. I never for a second imagined that salt could take what I had just tasted and turn it from blah to brilliant. That is the power of salt.

But I didn't throw the soup out. I figured, what can I lose—I'll just keep adding salt and see what happens. I'd add, stir, taste. Nothing. And repeat. Until finally, a wisp of something: a carrot, a hint of fennel, the deep earthy and caramel notes of the roasted bones. The flavor would begin on the front of my tongue and with each addition of salt fill in the middle of my palate, extend to the back of my tongue, and linger at the finish. When the soup was "there" I could literally taste all of the work, all of the extra time and technique. How many people have eaten or thrown away their disappointing dish, not knowing that more salt, patience, and tasting would have transformed it right under their noses? It was, eventually, an amazing soup—the best matzo ball soup I'd ever had with one exception: it was not cooked and served to me by Gummy. To experience the glory of that soup for yourself, see the recipe on page 32.

TASTES LIKE THE OCEAN

There are two types of people in the world: those who are comfortable with a little ambiguity and those who most definitely are not. The latter type need everything spelled out and explained to the letter. This can cause anxiety when it comes to an instruction such as "to taste."

Most people fall somewhere in the middle of the bell curve, flip-flopping back and forth between comfort and distress with ambiguity, depending on their mood. When I'm in the kitchen, I tend to eschew things like measuring spoons and instead cook by feel and experience. I have, at times, conveyed this laid-back logic to non-cooks. I once told a friend to make sure the cooking water for blanching string beans "tasted like the ocean." Normally, I'm never questioned about what this specifically means. People get the idea of it: *OK, make it taste really salty* and then off they go. But have I mentioned that this friend is an ocean physicist?

Telling her to make something "taste like the ocean" held no water. She emailed back: "A rough number for open ocean salinity is 35 parts per thousand (ppt). 4 quarts of water is about 4 liters, so 1 ppt = 4 ml and 35 ppt = 140 ml. There's about 5 milliliters per teaspoon and 3 teaspoons per tablespoon, so that's 9 or 10 tablespoons of salt. You want me to put 10 tablespoons of salt in the pot? That's a lot!"

So I got on the phone and told her that, yeah, maybe telling her to make something taste like the ocean was a bad choice on my part. Thinking I was clever, I told her to make it taste like brackish water—Puget Sound perhaps.

"Well, Puget Sound is more like 25 parts per thousand," she said, "so that would be about 7 tablespoons of salt in the pot, is that what you meant?" "Uh," I replied, "just put 2 tablespoons of kosher salt in your pot."

Later that day she left me a voicemail: "You should tell people to make the water taste like the Baltic Sea between Sweden and Germany."

Experiment Time

Lesson: Learn how salt is the conductor of a dish, bringing together and balancing all the disparate players.

Careful readers will note that I'm a little gaga about all the positives that the right amount of salt bestows onto your food. However, there is nothing like experiencing it firsthand to make the lesson stick. If salt is this important, what happens if you leave it completely out of the recipe (assuming you're not someone who cooks without it)? Allow me to show you. In the following experimental recipe, follow the directions carefully. I will be leading you through the preparation of a salad that eventually will taste good (have faith), but along the way, without salt's magical powers lending a hand, it will taste impressively not. Grab a notepad and a pen because I'll be asking you to jot down some thoughts. After you've tasted the food and considered each question, read my comments to see what most people experience at that stage of the taste experiment.

This is the most important experiment in the whole book. Get right with salt and all the rest falls into place. You'll never think about it the same way again!

Spiced Carrot Salad MAKES 4 SERVINGS

- 1 pound carrots (choose the best, freshest, tops-on carrots you can find, preferably local), peeled if not organic
- ½ teaspoon cumin seeds
- 1 (1-inch) piece cinnamon stick
- 1 teaspoon sweet or smoked paprika
- ¼ cup extra-virgin olive oil
- 3 tablespoons freshly squeezed lemon juice, plus more to taste

- Up to 2 teaspoons fine sea salt
- 1 teaspoon honey (optional)
- ¼ cup goat cheese (chèvre)
- ¼ cup chopped fresh Italian parsley
- 1 tablespoon minced serrano chile (seeds and membranes removed unless you like it hot)
- 1 teaspoon freshly grated ginger
- ¼ cup toasted pumpkin seeds, for garnish

1 First taste a bite of carrot on its own. Note how sweet or earthy it is and whether there are any bitter notes.

Becky says: *Most people will detect a bit of sweetness at the front of the tongue and, after swallowing, some might experience a lingering hint of bitterness after 5 to 10 seconds. (See page 8 for an explanation of how genetics might affect your ability to taste.)*

2 Grate the carrots on the coarse side of a box grater or in a food processor and place in a bowl. You should have about 4 cups.

3 In a dry medium skillet over medium-high heat, toast the cumin seeds and cinnamon stick until the seeds start to brown and smell aromatic, about 1 minute. Using your hands, break the cinnamon into smaller pieces and combine with the cumin and paprika in a spice grinder or mortar bowl. Grind the spices to a fine powder (pass through a fine mesh strainer to remove any bigger pieces of cinnamon that may not have been ground all the way, especially if you are grinding by hand). Don't they smell great?

4 Sprinkle the spice mixture over the grated carrots and toss very well to incorporate. Now taste a carrot piece or two. What the heck is going on in your mouth? Describe the texture. How did the spices affect the sweetness of the carrot?

Becky says: *Pretty terrible, huh? Cursing my name about now? Without salt, the spices accentuate any dry or earthy notes in the carrot, completely obliterating the natural sweetness. The spices overpower and create a dreadful imbalance on the palate.*

5 If I forbid you from adding salt to fix the dish at this point, what would you add instead? Fat? Acid? Try fat first. Test the theory by stirring the olive oil into the carrots thoroughly and then taste. What happens?

Becky says: *Fat will both coat the palate and carry flavor (see Chapter 5 for more information), but the unique properties of olive oil may or may not add bitterness and acidity as well. The dish will likely be greasy, perhaps more bitter, and some of the spice will recede a little. The moisture of the fat will help the texture a bit, but all in all, it will still taste terrible. You may begin to notice emptiness in your mid-palate.*

6 Time to test the acid theory. Add the lemon juice to the bowl, mix well, and taste again.

Becky says: *OK, we are starting to get somewhere. The acid is clearly balancing the fat and lifting the energy of the dish (see Chapter 3 for more on this), but at this exact moment you should really detect the bottom falling out at the center of your tongue. The dish doesn't taste horrid anymore but there is no soul; there is a distinct drop-off of flavor, no finish, and a lack of unity among all the disparate players.*

7 Now it's time to add salt. Start with ¼ teaspoon fine sea salt. Mix well and taste. I'm specifically having you hold back to tease the palate a little bit. Observe that hypothetical hole in the middle of the tongue slowly filling in. Keep stirring in salt just ¼ teaspoon at a time and tasting after each addition. When you can taste the salad consistently from the front of your tongue to the back, you've added enough. Listen to any "mmm's" that you may start to make (of course, not everyone will love this salad, so don't feel bad if you don't). When you've added the proper amount of salt, you should notice that the carrot flavor is back. If you initially detected any bitterness, it should have receded a bit due to the magic bitter-busting effects of salt. If the salad is still a bit bitter, stir in the honey for some sweetness.

8 Finally, it's gravy time: add the goat cheese, parsley, chile, and ginger. The salt brought together the disparate elements; the cheese, herbs, aromatics, and heat from the chile are all extras to create further interest but aren't crucial to the dish. Once you learn to identify when salt is missing, you should always start with that before reaching for other ingredients. Taste the salad again to make sure the added ingredients didn't tilt the balance in an undesirable direction. If you want more brightness, add more lemon juice, but keep in mind that acid turns down the perception of salt, so retaste it afterward—you might need a bit more salt for balance. Garnish with the pumpkin seeds just before serving.

Note: *Try this salad as an accompaniment to roast or grilled lamb.*

Ode to Gummy's Matzo Ball Soup MAKES 6 SERVINGS

The quality of this soup rests on the back of the stock that you use (and whether—unlike me—you remember to add salt to the soup). Follow the recipe on page 34. You can make the stock up to a week ahead and leave in the fridge or up to six months ahead if you freeze it in quart containers. To thaw, simply place the container in a bowl of warm water. When you can dislodge the stock, dump it into a pot and bring to a boil before reusing. Head here to watch me cut up a chicken: bit.ly/2qGBA0p.

For the matzo balls:
- 4 eggs, lightly beaten
- 1 cup Manischewitz matzo meal (some habits die hard, including using Gummy's favorite brand)
- ¼ cup vegetable oil or, better yet, chicken fat (schmaltz)
- 1 quart plus ¼ cup Roasted Chicken Stock (recipe follows), divided
- 2 quarts water
- 1½ tablespoons kosher salt

For the soup:
- About 2 quarts (enough to cover chicken) Roasted Chicken Stock (recipe follows)
- 1 bunch Italian parsley, stems reserved and leaves roughly chopped
- 5 stems fresh thyme
- 2 teaspoons fine sea salt
- 1 teaspoon fennel seeds (optional)
- ¼ teaspoon red pepper flakes (optional)
- Bone-in breasts, legs, and thighs from 1 chicken
- 1 large onion, cut into medium dice
- 4 stalks celery, sliced into ¼-inch half-moons
- 2 medium carrots, halved lengthwise and sliced into ¼-inch half-moons
- ½ cup fennel, cut into small dice (optional)
- Freshly ground black pepper

1 To make the matzo balls, follow the directions on the matzo meal box by beating the eggs in a medium bowl. Add the oil or schmaltz to the eggs, along with the matzo meal and ¼ cup

of the chicken stock. Mix until uniform, cover lightly, and chill for 20 minutes in the refrigerator. Scoop out small ice cream–ball pieces of the matzo meal mixture, and, using lightly damp hands, form them into approximately 1-inch balls, being careful to handle them gently to avoid making them tough. Set aside while you heat up the stock/water mixture.

2 Combine the remaining 1 quart chicken stock along with the water in a large pot over high heat. Add the kosher salt. Bring to a boil. Reduce to a simmer, gently add the matzo balls, and cover. Simmer for 30 to 40 minutes, or until the balls are cooked to your preferred doneness—some like them very soft and fluffy throughout, others like them a little bit chewier and less done in the center.

3 To make the soup, heat the chicken stock in a large pot over medium-high heat. Add the parsley stems, thyme, sea salt, fennel seeds, and red pepper flakes. Adjust the heat to maintain a bare simmer. Carefully lower the chicken legs and thighs into the stock and cook, covered, with the lid slightly ajar. After 30 minutes, add the breasts and cook for another 10 to 15 minutes, or until the chicken is cooked through (check with a knife).

4 Strain the broth, discarding the parsley and thyme. Set the chicken aside to cool and reheat the strained broth over medium-high heat. Add the onion, celery, carrots, and fennel to the pot. Bring the soup to a boil, then reduce to maintain a gentle simmer.

5 Meanwhile, pull the chicken meat off the bones and shred it. Add the chicken and parsley leaves to the soup and check the seasonings. Adjust the flavor of the soup with sea salt and add black pepper if desired. Put 3 to 4 matzo balls in each person's bowl and ladle the soup over the top, making sure each portion has a bit of the chicken.

●~~~~~~▶

Roasted Chicken Stock MAKES 5 QUARTS

- 1 chicken carcass (breasts, legs, and thighs removed for the soup or another use) plus 1 pound necks or backs
- 2 leeks, white and light-green parts only, halved lengthwise and cleaned well
- 1 large yellow onion, quartered
- 4 carrots, left whole
- 4 stalks celery, left whole
- Tops and fronds from 1 fennel bulb, left whole
- 10 sprigs fresh thyme
- 10 sprigs fresh Italian parsley
- 2 dried bay leaves
- 10 black peppercorns
- 2 gallons cold water
- Splash of dry white wine

1 Preheat the oven to 450 degrees F.

2 Place the chicken carcass, necks, and backs on a large baking sheet and roast until browned, about 45 minutes. Add the leeks, onion, carrots, celery, fennel, thyme, parsley, and bay, and toss them with the chicken fat. Roast for another 20 minutes.

3 Transfer everything to a large pot with the peppercorns and cover with the water. Place over high heat. Meanwhile, set the baking sheet over low heat and add the wine while scraping up all the good brown bits. Pour this liquid gold into the pot, scraping off every last speck. (Use a little water if you need more deglazing liquid.)

4 When bubbles begin to break the surface of the stock, turn the heat down to medium-low to maintain a very gentle simmer. Cook, uncovered, for 3 to 4 hours, skimming any scum from the surface with a spoon or fine-mesh strainer every 10 to 15 minutes for the first hour of cooking and occasionally as it develops over the next few hours. (This will help keep your stock from clouding.) Add hot water as needed to keep the bones and vegetables submerged. Enjoy the smell of your house.

5 Strain the stock through a fine-mesh strainer into another large stockpot or heatproof container. Discard the solids. Return the stock to the stove and reduce for another 30 minutes to concentrate the flavors. Cool the stock immediately to below 40 degrees F by placing the pot into a large cooler of ice water or a sink full of ice water. Cover and refrigerate overnight. Remove and discard solidified fat from the surface. Store the stock in an airtight container in the refrigerator for up to 1 week or in the freezer for up to 6 months. Prior to use, bring to a boil for 2 minutes.

Chapter Three

ACID

t's the heat of summer, 99 degrees and sticky humid, and you've been working outside. A little kid sells you a cup of lemonade for $4.50 (because inflation). You tip it back, guzzling the whole thing in one long pull. How do you feel? Most people would say refreshed. When you eat or drink something refreshing, I bet acidity is in play. In fact, if your food is sour, tangy, sharp, lifting, quenching, bright, sunny, salivating, light, or tart, I'd put money on it. Acidity energizes food and wakes you up, slapping you out of a culinary deep sleep. It's a cold splash of water on your face and the brightness of the afternoon sun in your eyes. Without acidity, food might feel heavy, lifeless, leaden, dull, and overly rich. It's the main reason my mid-August beef broth stand never took off.

We spent a lot of time talking about salt because it's so important in making great food, but nipping at salt's heels in terms of importance is acidity, or the sourness that comes from vinegar, wine, and citrus. In restaurant kitchens I've worked in, the two most likely things barked from chef to cook refer to salt and acid. If you had been a fly on the wall when I was a line cook at the Herbfarm Restaurant in Woodinville, Washington, this is what you'd have heard: "needs salt," "add lemon juice," "it's too salty," "bump up the acidity," or "hit it with vinegar"—in addition to a bunch of other comments I cannot in good conscience print in this book. Very rarely would it be: "I think this needs saffron" or "It's good but there's a definite lack of paprika." Once you've solved for salt, head straight to nailing down the proper amount of acidity in a dish. Correctly deployed, acidity can make both food and beverage absolutely sing.

Acid 101

Super simply stated, when you eat something acidic, hydrogen ions cause taste cells to fire, release neurotransmitters, and alert your brain that you have ingested something sour. A little bit of acidity goes a long way. Our taste buds are highly sensitive to sour foods (as well as bitter ones). A little hit of sour is refreshing, but too much points to a potential lack of ripeness (in fruit) or, at the other end of the spectrum, spoilage (think milk past its prime).

> **FUN FACT** My own anecdotal observations of pockets of children seem to show that they really like sour stuff, as evidenced by the extremely sour candy they consume: Warheads, Zotz, Zours, Sour Patch Kids, AirHeads Xtremes. A 2003 study found that, indeed, children in the United States and United Kingdom are much more likely to prefer sour foods than adults.[10]

Acidity also makes you salivate. Without saliva, you can't taste much of anything. Imagine (or if you're really committed, do it) drying off your tongue with an absorbent towel and then putting a small piece of pizza on your tongue. You will taste little to nothing without saliva to ferry the compounds to your taste buds.

Not every dish needs acidity, but acidity should absolutely be a part of every meal, either via an accompanying dish (such as a pickled item) or a beverage. Imagine a typical Midwestern beef stew with chunks of beef chuck, potatoes, celery, and carrots. It was probably made with beef stock. Some stews include tomatoes, which would be a source of acid, but most do not. Without the acidity of tomatoes in the stew, what beverage do you think you'd crave along with it? If you answered beer or wine, the wisdom of your palate was speaking for you. If you don't drink alcohol, carbonated water is slightly acidic and will lift and perk up a heavy, rich dish.

DECIPHERING AN ACID PROBLEM

When food is lacking acidity you may detect the following:
- What wine experts refer to as "flabbiness"; a cloying, syrupy sensation
- Greasiness on the lips (imagine an overly oily salad dressing)
- Dullness or a sensation of lifelessness
- Too little saliva in your mouth

Using Acidity to Balance a Dish

The more savory a dish, the greater the need for some acidity to perk it up. Mushrooms, meat, and beans really do well with a hit of acid. A splash of white wine with mushrooms, a hit of sherry vinegar to finish off beans, tomatoes to cut through a fatty beef dish. Cloyingly sweet dishes also benefit greatly from the addition of acidity. Sour cream or mascarpone added to whipped cream and paired with a rich, sweet chocolate cake; a squirt of lemon juice mixed into raspberry or peach puree. Acidity can affect the mouthfeel of a dish, turning something fatty and/or meaty into something balanced (tangy ketchup on a burger or tart cranberry sauce on a roast turkey sandwich). One of acid's greatest tricks is its ability to turn down our perception of salt. If your "pinch" of salt got a little out of control, try adding acidity and taste it again.

MIRACLE BERRY AND FLAVOR-TRIPPING

Miracle berry comes from miracle fruit—otherwise known as *Synsepalum dulcificum*, a plant native to West Africa. Within the berry is a protein called miraculin, which, while sounding like a Harry Potter spell, can switch your perception of sour things into sweet things (known as flavor-tripping). Bitter foods also taste sweeter due to the taste receptor–blocking effects of miraculin. Drink pure lemon juice and be stunned when it tastes exactly like sweet lemon pie. Tabasco turns into hot donut glaze. Goat cheese becomes cheesecake. Flavor-tripping parties were all the rage around the time the *New York Times* published a story on them in 2008, at which you'd consume miracle berry at the door and then eat your way through a pile of foods you'd never enjoy on their own. If you are tempted to try miracle berry, go easy. Things might taste sweet, but your body will ultimately reject large amounts of lemon juice and hot sauce. Have Tums on hand.

Unlike different kinds of unflavored salts, which (with some caveats) essentially season your food the same way, if you're cooking with ingredients such as vinegar or citrus fruit, you bring other flavors to the dish along with the acidity. This, consequently, is considered a disadvantage in the processed food world where they want to be able to manipulate acidity, fat, and umami without affecting the flavor of the food (see the discussion of MSG on page 102). Cooking with whole foods means you often get additional flavor with the basic taste. I think of this as an advantage to the cook and it leads to endless variations in the kitchen. Sherry vinegar does more than simply alter the pH of the dish—it also adds woodsy depth and nuttiness and is fabulous paired with nuts and beans. Light, crisp rice vinegar goes beautifully with cool green cucumbers.

My friend Kim Brauer, author of *The No-Bullshit Guide to Succeeding in Culinary School*, is obsessed with lemons. When we cook together, I have to stay alert because she is always throwing a lemon at me—sometimes literally. I credit her for teaching me to sometimes double down on acid and mix lemon juice with a little bit of vinegar to get the sunny sweet-sour note of the citrus along with earthy, apple, or wine notes of a vinegar for greater complexity. For example, if you toss roasted beets (a notoriously earthy and sweet vegetable that some might say tastes like soil) with just lemon juice, olive oil, and salt, it would no doubt be good, but if you supplement the sunny lemon juice with a tiny splash of sherry vinegar for its woodsy earthiness, you get a roasted beet dish that is far more complex and delicious than if you had used only one or the other. In fact, when I've tried just using sherry vinegar with roasted beets, it didn't work; the earthiness was overpowering and all you tasted was the sherry. When I gave samples to chef friends of roasted beets with either just lemon juice, lemon juice and sherry vinegar, just sherry vinegar, or a sweet balsamic vinegar, the lemon-vinegar combo was universally selected as the best. The balsamic alone, by the way, was too cloying.

WAYS ACIDITY ACCOMPANIES VARIOUS CUISINES:

- Pickled ginger to be eaten as a palate cleanser between bites of fatty sashimi or sushi
- A bright and refreshing sorbet served in the middle of a multi-course tasting menu (it resets the palate, reenergizing you for the coming courses)
- Kimchi with fatty pork
- Japanese pickles with rich dishes, such as pickled cucumbers or daikon radish
- Sauerkraut with heavy meat dishes, such as bratwurst
- Lemons offered with fried fish to cut the fattiness
- Ketchup on starchy potatoes (or really everything)

Sometimes a dish has enough acidity but you want to bump up the perception of brightness without overwhelming the palate and unbalancing the dish. One option is to add finely grated citrus zest (keeping in mind that you may also be introducing some bitterness from any white pith that sneaks in). Or, instead, reach for lemongrass and lime leaf—both will convey the brightness of citrus without the high level of acidity.

Ways to Fix an Overly Acidic Dish

1   Add some sweetness in the form of sugar, honey, dried fruit, etc. Thinking back to the lemonade example, we know that adding sugar to lemonade cuts down our perception of its acidity.

2   Add fat to "coat the tongue" and interrupt the assault of acidity (think of how you balance a vinaigrette). This works well in cases such as where you accidentally dumped ½ cup of vinegar into a stew and you don't want to add a lot of sugar to balance it.

3   Add bulk or dilute by adding more protein, vegetables, or anything not acidic to spread the acidity out. Water or stock work as well. Just remember to retaste afterward to make sure you haven't swung the pendulum in a different direction.

4   Try any combination of 1, 2, and 3 if one on its own isn't doing the trick.

MY DAD SUCKS LEMONS

My dad sucks lemons, or at least he used to. We all know this weird fact in my family. I try, with little success, to picture my six-foot-tall father, '70s Tom Selleck 'stache and all, as a little boy running around the house while sucking on a lemon. My grandparents thought it was strange behavior but figured it kept him off the harder stuff, like pure citric acid. If you're to believe my grandmother, my dad had a frog in his hand, rocks and shells in his pockets, and a lemon in his mouth 24-7. Growing up, I never noticed my adult father sucking lemons. I figured he must have moved beyond his childhood addiction until one day when he let me try a sip of his most favorite wine, Pinot Grigio. As crisp and refreshing as lemonade, Pinot Grigio is the adult version of lemon-sucking—just add alcohol.

I inherited his love of acidity, if not his love of frogs. I had a particular affinity for an off-label use of Country Time lemonade flavor drink mix. I would eat it straight from the cylinder, using my questionably clean finger as a dipping stick. Put aside your disgust that unaware adults would use that same contaminated beverage mix for their summertime drinks, and appreciate the hyper-hit of sour and sweet that drew me into the safety of the dark pantry, day after day, when no one was paying attention. Don't feel sorry for the latchkey kids of the '70s—we were too busy being up to no good to feel sorry for ourselves.

If my stash at home ran out, I'd walk the half mile down the road to my grandmother's house where I'd find Gummy in the kitchen holding a cheap serrated paring knife in her hand, slicing lemons on the built-in cutting board, worn down from years of use to a wobbly quarter-inch-thick piece of warped wood. She'd carefully slice the lemon into wheels, destined for the forest-green cut-glass iced-tea pitcher. "You know," she would tell me for the fiftieth time, "your father used to suck lemons."

Not All Acidic Things Are Equal

Culinary myths makes me stabby with rage, and the commonly held belief that vinaigrettes should have a 3:1 ratio of fat to acid is one of them. Which form of acidity you use makes a difference in this ratio. Vinegars have a wide range of acetic acid levels. Japanese rice vinegar can be as low as 4 percent, cider vinegars are typically around 5 percent, and wine vinegars can be as high as 7 percent. The acid in lemon or lime juice is citric acid, not acetic acid, and the pH is slightly lower. Saying 3:1 is easy to remember but too simplistic to take into account the varieties and differences in acid types and the wealth of possible acidic ingredients you can use in a vinaigrette.

Whichever acid you end up using in a vinaigrette, whether it be lemon or white wine vinegar or both, use your senses to determine the perfect ratio. If the dressing is greasy and oil coats your lips, there is too much fat. If you cough and the sharpness of the acid makes you pucker, there's too much acidity. A perfectly balanced vinaigrette is just fatty enough to leave a light sheen on your lips and acidic enough to be refreshingly bright, causing your mouth to water slightly.

Experiment Time

Lesson: Discover how acidity can cut richness and add brightness and energy to a salad.

Salsa verde is both a Mexican green salsa with a base of tomatillos and cilantro as well as an Italian sauce featuring herbs, capers, olive oil, and garlic. Below is my version of the latter, and it is fantastic with, well, almost everything but especially grilled meats, fish, eggplant, beans, and potatoes. One great use of the sauce is as a dressing for the white bean and charred radicchio salad on page 90. As with other recipe experiments, I'll be asking you to add ingredients progressively and then taste. If you'd like, reserve a small bit at each stage so you can go back and revisit how the flavors have developed and changed.

Italian Salsa Verde MAKES 1 CUP

- 1 cup loosely packed, roughly chopped Italian parsley (stems are fine)
- ½ cup extra-virgin olive oil, plus more as needed
- 1 medium or 2 small oil-packed anchovies
- 1 small clove garlic, roughly chopped

- 2 teaspoons raisins or zante currants
- 5 toasted whole almonds
- ¼ teaspoon red pepper flakes
- ¼ teaspoon fine sea salt
- 1 teaspoon capers
- 2 to 3 tablespoons sherry vinegar

1 Place the first eight ingredients (everything but the capers and vinegar) into a blender and process until the puree is a vibrant green. If you have any problems getting the blender to operate because there is not enough liquid in the jar to get it going, add more olive oil, 1 tablespoon at a time, until the blender runs smoothly.

2 Taste the puree and make note of how your lips feel. Think about how you would describe the energy of the dish: earthy and heavy, neutral and balanced, or bright, light, and perky.

Becky says: *The good news is that you won't need lip balm for a few days because I bet your lips are greasy as hell right now. We all love fat, but too much of a good thing isn't so good at all and at this point the salsa verde is heavy, rich, and lacking in energy. There is acidity in olive oil but not enough to balance it out.*

3 OK, it's time to add some acidity. Start with the capers, which are a crossover ingredient in that they are both salty and acidic (and even contain a little umami). Add them to the blender and

process. Using a rubber spatula, scrape out the vibrant green puree into a bowl and give it a taste.

Becky says: *Adding capers will boost the salt content, which, as covered in Chapter 2, may turn down any bitter notes from the olive oil. The acidity of the capers will also cut the richness, but only ever so slightly because there aren't a lot of them. You should still detect the greasiness and heaviness of the fat, just a bit less so.*

4 Now stir in 2 tablespoons of the sherry vinegar and taste again. Jot down your thoughts, paying attention to how your lips feel, how you would express the earthiness or brightness, and if you detect any catch in your throat. Is your mouth watering at all?

Becky says: *The sherry vinegar, though earthier than, say, white distilled vinegar, is nonetheless capable of balancing the fat, raising the energy of the sauce, and creating some balance where little existed before. Salsa verde is a sauce, but it is also frequently used like a salad dressing, and good salad dressings are bright and acidic to help cleanse the palate. Does this sauce taste cloying or exciting to you? You should find that it is bright, refreshing, and quite complex, perhaps even a touch too acidic on its own (but won't be once added to a salad). If your lips still feel greasy, add a little more vinegar, 1 teaspoon at a time, until there is a nice balance between richness and brightness.*

Salmon with Miso Vinaigrette and Sesame-Roasted Vegetables MAKES 4 SERVINGS

I include this recipe in the acid chapter because the vinaigrette, with its double dose of acidity from the yogurt and sauerkraut, combines with the miso to create a surprisingly round and refreshing counterbalance to the richness of the salmon. Bonus points for slipping some healthy probiotics into the meal. Don't tell your guests what's in the dressing; make them guess.

For the roasted vegetables:
- 1 large unpeeled sweet potato, cut into large dice
- 1 large fennel bulb, cut crosswise into ¼-inch slices
- 1 leek, white and light-green parts only, cut into ¼-inch rounds
- 1 cup coarsely chopped red cabbage
- 1 tablespoon toasted sesame oil
- 1 tablespoon seasoned rice vinegar
- 2 teaspoons fish sauce
- ½ teaspoon red pepper flakes
- ¼ teaspoon fine sea salt

For the miso vinaigrette:
- ½ cup sauerkraut (made from green cabbage, not red)
- ½ cup extra-virgin olive oil
- ¼ cup full-fat Greek yogurt
- ¼ cup water
- 2 tablespoons white miso paste
- 2 teaspoons soy sauce

For the salmon:
- 1 tablespoon high-heat oil, such as avocado, or high-heat fat, such as ghee
- 1 pound wild salmon, skin-on, cut into 4 (4-ounce) portions
- ½ teaspoon fine sea salt
- 2 teaspoons chile oil (see Note), for garnish (optional)

●~~~~~►

1 To make the roasted vegetables, first preheat the oven to 400 degrees F and line a baking sheet with parchment paper. In a large bowl, toss the vegetables with the sesame oil, rice vinegar, fish sauce, red pepper flakes, and salt. Transfer to the baking sheet and roast for 20 to 25 minutes, stirring halfway through, until tender and charred in places.

2 While the vegetables are cooking, make the vinaigrette. Pulse all of the ingredients together in a blender until smooth. Store extra dressing in an airtight container in the refrigerator for up to 2 weeks.

3 To make the salmon, in a nonstick pan (I prefer seasoned cast-iron), heat the oil over high heat. Season the salmon with salt and place the fillets in the pan skin side down, pressing lightly on the fish to help the skin crisp up. To see me demonstrate this technique, visit bit.ly/2p9WzbB. After a few minutes, check to see that the skin is crispy and then flip the salmon pieces over. Place the pan on the center rack of the oven and cook until the salmon is medium rare in the center (125 to 130 degrees F). Alternatively, continue cooking on the stovetop over medium-low heat.

4 Serve the salmon over the vegetables, drizzling 2 to 3 tablespoons of vinaigrette around each plate. Garnish the dish with a few drops of chile oil.

Note: *To make chile oil at home, in a small saucepan over medium heat, combine 1 cup peanut oil with 3 to 5 tablespoons red pepper flakes (depending on how spicy you want the oil to be). Heat the oil until it reaches 300 degrees F on an instant-read thermometer. Remove the pan from the heat and try not to breathe in the fumes! Once the oil cools to 250 degrees F, add 1 tablespoon toasted sesame oil. Strain the oil and store it in an airtight container in the refrigerator, where it will keep for many months.*

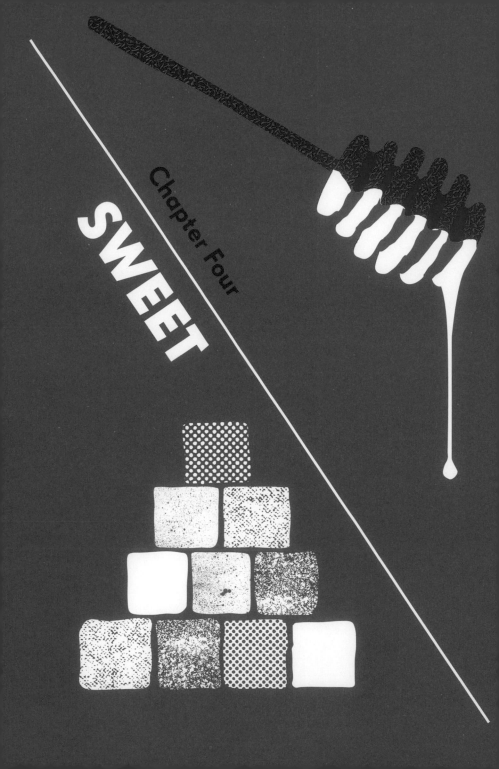

Chapter Four

SWEET

We are sugar-seekers by evolutionary design. Sugar is nature's caloric neon sign. Where there is sugar, there is energy, and those who are best at finding it thrive, living longer to pass on their genes to the next generation of sugar-seekers. In today's world, we're extremely proficient at finding sugar. Piles and piles of it, in fact, with little hunting and gathering necessary. We are relatively desensitized to the stuff as compared to our sensitivity to bitter and sour substances. It takes us 1 part in 200 of sucrose in solution to recognize the sugar. By comparison, it only takes 1 part in 2 million for us to detect quinine—the bitter alkaloid found in the bark of the cinchona tree and used in tonic water—in solution. Sugar, in moderation, sustains us. Bitter makes us stop in our tracks and question if swallowing might kill us (see Chapter 6 for more on this).

Sweet 101

Sugar is a flavorant—like salt—in that it helps boost the flavors of food without adding extra flavors of its own (in the case of refined, granulated sugar). When you've made a dish that is consistent from the front of the palate to the back, with a long finish, the amount of salt is right. If the acidity is present, enlivening the flavors and cutting the fat, the dish is golden. But what if you still feel like something is lacking? It's time for a smidge of sweetness to lift all the other flavors. Just as you might not automatically think of adding a pinch of salt to a dessert (though you should!), using a pinch or drop of something sweet—or browning natural sugars in the presence of heat through caramelization—to enhance a savory dish is a tool in your bag that you can and should reach for.

There are many types of sweeteners to choose from, including everything from basic syrups to complex, chunky, and molasses-rich *jaggery* to man-made artificial sweeteners and many in between (I've included a list of my favorites on pages 54 to 55). Suffice it to say that all sugars, no matter the type, will activate your sweet taste receptors and shift the balance of the dish in a sweet direction.

Foods That Benefit from Sweetness

- Anything gamey or funky. Think of blue cheese with a bit of honey drizzled on it. Duck with orange. Lamb curry with cinnamon and caramelized onions.
- Acidic dishes. A pinch of sugar in spaghetti sauce is a classic example, used to balance acidic tomatoes that were not, on their own, as sweet as desired, or simply to boost the flavors of the sauce.
- Bitter foods. Radicchio is bitter as anything. Salting it will turn down the bitterness, but caramelizing it and drizzling with a bit of honey or sweet-sour balsamic vinegar is a great option as well.
- Salty foods. A little salt, we learned, turns up the perception of sweet things. But if something is really salty, besides upping the acidity, reach for something sweet. Think about a salty focaccia bread with caramelized onions on it. Sounds good, doesn't it? Prosciutto with a little bit of fig jam and perfectly ripe melon? Divine. And on the I'm-sure-I'm-not-alone front, how about dipping salty fries into a chocolate milkshake?

FUN FACT A 12-ounce can of regular Coke contains just over 3 tablespoons of sugar (39 grams). We all know sugar is addictive, and the Coca-Cola Company is smart (evil?) enough to use a high level of acidity in their beverages to counterbalance the sugar, masking how much is really in there. Coke tastes sweet but not so sickly sweet that it's widely rejected by adults. Also, cold beverages taste less sweet, so there is more sugar in Coke because it is meant to be consumed ice cold. If you've ever tasted a warm Coke, you might have noticed a more intense sweetness (and found it nearly unpalatable).

Swapping Sugars

You might think you could swap one type of sugar for another, as you might do with salts, but different sugars add more than sweetness alone. Only granulated sugar provides sweetness without aromatics (well, high-fructose corn syrup too, but you're unlikely to be cooking with that). All other sugars will affect the flavor balance of the food by contributing the unique properties they have to offer. Think about what a really floral honey would add to a cake recipe, or how using raisins as a sweetener might affect texture and flavor. Total aside: You must try Tupelo honey sometime in your life; it's incredible, with aromas of Earl Grey and flowers. It's not too sweet, just barely citrusy, and very clean tasting.

You might be wondering about the use of artificial sweeteners, and while I'm sentimental about the pink package of Sweet'N Low that my stepmother repetitively taps on her finger before adding it to her decaf coffee, I don't recommend them. Artificial sweeteners may or may not be harmful to us.[11] But more relevant to this book, they taste strange to most people, with bitter or metallic aftertastes that are difficult to mask. Obviously many diabetics rely on them to satisfy any sweet cravings, so for that reason, I'm glad there are options, but as a general practice I avoid using them.

I aim to use naturally occurring sugars more than refined sugars in my cooking, though I'm not rigid about this. I will roast and caramelize vegetables and use fruits and naturally sweet vinegars, such as balsamic, before reaching for granulated sugar. If fruit or balsamic vinegar just don't make sense in a dish, I will add some honey or maple syrup. Ultimately sugar is sugar is

SWEETENER SHORT LIST

Brown sugar: Many people don't realize that brown sugar is simply granulated sugar with molasses added in, making it deeper and slightly more complex in flavor. Light brown sugar has less molasses added to it than dark brown.

Coconut sugar: Less refined than granulated sugar, coconut sugar is made from the sap of flower buds from the coconut palm tree. The taste is similar to dark brown sugar.

Demerara sugar: Demerara is a partially refined, large grain cane sugar used for its naturally caramel-like flavor and crunchy texture. It's often used as a finishing sugar to provide texture and sweetness to a dessert, as in topping a cobbler or cookie.

Honey: The flavor of honey is as diverse as the plants from which bees harvest pollen, so it can't be qualified in any generalized way. The stronger the flavor of the honey, the less easily you'll be able to substitute it for granulated sugar.

Maple syrup: Maple syrup, made from tree sap, ranges from golden and delicate to very dark and strong. It's a perfect sweetener for pork or winter squashes and, combined with dark brown sugar, when making baked beans.

sugar to your body, but honey has aromatic qualities and antioxidants, which refined sugar does not. When baking, I love using a variety of sugars to add depth to the finished product. When you venture beyond granulated sugar, you can enjoy a world of sweetness with more complex flavor profiles.

Muscovado: This is a type of partially refined cane sugar with a strong molasses flavor. It is great paired with coffee or used in gingerbread.

Palm sugar: Used in Southeast Asian cuisine, palm sugar—made from tree flower sap—has a slightly toasty, smooth maple flavor.

Piloncillo: This unrefined whole cane sugar is commonly used in Mexico, often in moles, soups, and salsas. It's strong with a pleasant smoky molasses flavor. Piloncillo and jaggery, used in Asian cuisine, are very similar and can be used in place of each other.

Stevia: Stevia is an extremely sweet herb, but when refined it has a strange aftertaste. I don't use or recommend it.

Sucanat: Sucanat is a less refined granulated sugar that retains a higher proportion of molasses when compared to other types of cane sugars. It's intense and has a toasty, charred flavor.

Turbinado: A less processed cane sugar, turbinado comes from the first pressing of sugar cane and retains natural molasses. It can be used in place of brown sugar in baked goods, though you will be losing a small amount of the moisture that brown sugar contains. Simply add a drop of molasses or honey to compensate for the loss of moisture.

Sugar is a preservative (not necessarily of your teeth) because its greedy love for water means that it sucks the water out of microbe cell walls, causing them to dehydrate and die. That's why high-sugar jams are a pretty safe food to refrigerate, can, and freeze (though you still need to watch for mold).

Adding Sweetness without Sugar

The following are some options for taking advantage of natural flavors and ingredient properties that will satisfy cravings and/or provide balance in a dish.

- Use aromatics that remind you of sweet things, such as vanilla, unsweetened cocoa powder, and cinnamon. A dusting of cocoa or cinnamon in coffee tricks the palate into believing it's sweeter. You smell the cinnamon, think cinnamon roll, drink the coffee, and perceive it as sweeter.
- Use naturally sweet ingredients such as coconut milk, dates, dairy products such as plain yogurt or cream, or raisins (which I use in the Italian Salsa Verde recipe on page 45).
- Add a bit more salt to turn up the perception of sweetness in the dish. Test this for yourself by simply cutting an orange into cubes and dividing it among two bowls. Add the tiniest sprinkle of salt to one bowl, mix, and then compare the difference between the two. The salted orange should not taste salty—instead it should be clearly sweeter than the control.
- Roast vegetables to bring out more of their sweetness, or add some caramelized onions to a dish.

The Maillard Reaction and Caramelization

The Maillard reaction occurs when amino acids (protein) and a carbohydrate molecule react in the presence of heat, creating hundreds of new flavor molecules. The Maillard reaction is responsible for the flavor of roasted meats, bread crusts, roasted coffee (yes, there's some protein in coffee!), dark beers, and many other delicious foods. The difference in flavor between steak tartare and a grilled rib eye? The Maillard reaction! The difference between a slice of white bread and toast? The Maillard reaction!

Caramelization is a different and less complex process that occurs when sugars brown. For example, the natural sugars in vegetables undergo an incredible transformation when roasted—especially slightly bitter vegetables such as broccoli, brussels sprouts, and turnips—turning sweeter, nuttier, toastier, and more complex in flavor. This is what the king of food science, Harold McGee, has to say on the matter: "That's the magic of cooking front and center: from one odorless, colorless, simply sweet molecule, heat creates hundreds of different molecules, some aromatic and some tasty and some colored."

Think about the flavor of granulated sugar. It's a monotone, straightforward sweetness. There are no other flavors hitching a ride on the sweet train. Now, put that same sugar into a saucepan. Put the heat on, add a little water, and melt that sugar while swirling the pan. Watch it transform from white to transparent to tan to amber to a rich burnt umber. Once cool, give it a smell and a taste. That very same ingredient is completely transformed. One-dimensional sweetness has blossomed and deepened into a slightly bitter, toasty, smoky complex of flavors. How can this be the same ingredient? Such is the power of caramelization.

WHY SERVE DESSERT LAST?

Numerous theories abound as to why many cultures finish a meal with a bit of a sweet. Let's start with seventeenth-century Europe. Extreme hospitality made allowing anyone to leave a party unsatisfied or hungry scandalous, but tired staff wanted to leave after hours of entertainment marathons. Offering premade sweets set the tone for when the meal had ended, both gilding the lily and ensuring that no one was left wanting. The word "dessert" comes from the Old French *desservir*, which means "to clean the table."

A different take on the matter comes from the world of science: Norwegian researchers discovered that the ingestion of some sugar sends a message to your stuffed stomach to relax and allow just a bit more food in.[12] If you have children, do not share this next part with them: Science, therefore, lends credence to every child's claim that they still have some room in their stomach for dessert even if they couldn't finish their meal. A little bite of cake opens up enough space to allow us to finish the whole piece.

Sugar Adds So Much More Than Sweetness

I know I've been tempted to reduce the sugar in my baked goods, imagining that I could make brownies into something nearly healthy. But you must resist playing loose and free with sugar when baking because there will be unintended consequences. Ingredients can't simply be withheld or changed based on a whim, which is the entire reason pastry chefs tend to be rule followers and savory chefs are complete anarchists. Quite simply, you risk baking disaster when straying too far from a well-calibrated recipe. Sugar adds sweetness to baked goods but it also does the following:

1 It acts as a stabilizer. When making a meringue, as you whip air into egg whites, the proteins in the whites form a thin matrix that holds air pockets. This air bubble foam is kept stable by the sugar, making you less likely to overbeat the whites. Sugar also acts as the meringue's building engineer, preventing a structural collapse. The sugar dissolves into the water in the bubble's walls, forming a protective syrup that acts as support.

2 It provides texture. This can be in the form of crunchy turbinado or demerara sugar (see Chapter 10 for more information) or in the oven, when water evaporates from the surface of baked goods and the sugar recrystallizes. The latter is what gives you that crisp, shattery muffin top or the crackly crust on brownies that I pick off (because *hello!* it's the best part).

3 It keeps your sweet treats moist and tender. Sugar is hydrophilic, which is a fancy way of saying that sugar really loves water. Without the proper amount of sugar on board the water is all, "See ya!" It's a package deal. Because of this lovefest between sugar and water, if there is less sugar in the batter, the proteins and complex starches get greedy for the available water. Gluten needs water to really get going. Want a donut with the texture of a bagel? Reduce the sugar in the recipe.

4 It acts as a leavener. Sugar cuts into the mixture of fat, eggs, and other liquids and creates thousands of tiny air bubbles. These bubbles expand and lift baked goods. Without them, say hello to sad, flat, pucklike biscuits. Poor sad, flat, pucklike biscuits.

5 It contributes to browning and deeper flavor development through caramelization. Think of the flavor difference between a marshmallow out of the bag and a toasted one.

But what about switching out "solid" sugars, such as granulated, for liquid ones, such as maple syrup or honey? Things can get tricky. Not only is there a major flavor addition with this substitution, but both maple syrup and honey are sweeter than granulated sugar, so you need less. For every cup of granulated sugar, you should only use ½ to ¾ cup of honey or maple syrup. Keep in mind you are also introducing liquid that the recipe didn't account for, so you'll have to reduce the amount of other liquid in the recipe proportionate to the replacement sweetener—about 25 percent liquid reduction in relation to the amount of sweetener added is a rough estimate. Honey and maple syrup are also slightly acidic, so you would need to counter this by adding some (or more) baking soda. Furthermore, honey and maple syrup caramelize faster than granulated sugar, so the oven temperature needs to be reduced accordingly. Is it starting to become obvious why I don't think it's a great idea to fuss too much with baking recipes unless you're a pastry professional?

Caveat: If you are an avid baker who wants to play around with recipes, you should dig deep into the chemistry of baking. I've included some fantastic references for you in the Bibliography on page 216. If this whole baking discussion—and its requisite perfectly measured ingredients and cautionary advice on creative recipe alterations—has made you twitchy, then I welcome you into my anarchist band of savory chefs. We pride ourselves on our ability to wing it.

How to Fix an Oversweetened Dish

1 Add bulk or dilute: distribute the sweetness over a larger volume of ingredients. Add water, more meat, or more vegetables.

2 Add acidity to counterbalance the sweetness. Dollop some sour cream or yogurt (both acidic) on top of a sweet potato soup or borscht. If you don't want highly flavored acidity

in a dish, you can use distilled white vinegar or citric acid (which is sold in bulk in many stores).

3   Add heat, as in chiles and other "bitey" ingredients (see Chapter 9 for ideas). Sweet and hot balance each other out.

4   Add fat to coat the palate and suppress the perception of sweetness.

5   Avoid adding more salt, as salt enhances the perception of sweetness.

My Name Is Becky, and I'm Addicted to Sugar

Does sugar have you trapped in its sweet, addictive embrace? You are not alone. I co-teach a class called "Food as Medicine" with my colleague and friend Dr. Tanmeet Sethi, a family physician faculty attending at Swedish Family Medicine Residency in Seattle. We met through a mutual friend and quickly discovered that I wanted to be a doctor and she wanted to be a chef. She is the creator and director of the residency program's Integrative Medicine fellowship, through which she teaches doctors to consider nutrition and mind-body medicine, among other things, as an integral part of a primary care practice.

Beyond that, she has helped me battle my addiction to sugar. Here's the basic idea: I, cold turkey, cut out sugar for ten days. Her plan is not as restrictive as some others in that you are allowed to eat fruit and drink alcohol because she wants you to be successful and recognizes that humans are not *robots*. What's amazing is that when you get through the ten days without sugar in your coffee, without pastries or processed foods, without sodas or juices, without candy, you eat a cookie and suddenly it's ridiculously, obnoxiously sweet. Your new taste buds are super sensitized to the sugar now that you haven't been bathing your tongue with the stuff on a daily basis. This is the critical time to rewire how you approach your dysfunctional relationship with sugar.

Once I finished my sugar fast, I celebrated with a chocolate chip cookie (to test my taste buds), and something miraculous happened that has never ever happened in the history of me and a chocolate chip cookie. I ate half of it, slowly, and then carefully wrapped up the other half and—I still can't believe it—ate it later. The trick is to not slide face first back into a pile of pastries and undo the innocence of those fresh taste buds. Just as soon as I finish this bag of gummy bears, I'll write more about what happens when you're weak and succumb to the many sugary temptations that pop up in your life at each turn.

Wine Pairing and Sweetness

I reached out to my friend Master Sommelier Emily Wines (yes, I know, she was born to do this) for some guidance about when to serve sweet or off-dry (lightly sweet) wines. Sugar can act as a sensory distraction to the palate when paired with really spicy food, so a sweeter wine provides delicious relief during a fiery feast. "This mixture of pain and pleasure," says Wines, "is the reason there are so many sweet and hot dishes out there." So if you're eating a five-star Thai curry, a semi-sweet, low-alcohol Riesling will be a good match; the sweetness and aromatics are going to distract and comfort your fiery palate. (Check out page 189 to see why a high-alcohol wine would exacerbate the fire.) Master Sommelier Chris Tanghe added, "You always want your wine to be sweeter or as sweet as what you are eating." If you pair a sweet dessert with a dry wine, the sweetness in the food is going to make the wine taste less fruit-forward, one note, acidic, lean, or thin.

Experiment Time

Lesson: Demonstrate how salt and aromatics make bitter coffee seem sweeter without actually adding anything sweet.

Materials needed: Three mugs, 12 ounces of strong, dark roast coffee, ¼ teaspoon unsweetened cocoa powder, ¼ teaspoon ground cinnamon, vanilla extract, fine sea salt, and an unwitting partner.

Method: Divide the coffee among the three mugs and make sure your partner isn't watching. In the first mug, do nothing to the coffee—this is your control. In the second mug, stir in the following: ¼ teaspoon unsweetened cocoa powder, ¼ teaspoon ground cinnamon, and 1 to 2 drops vanilla extract. In the third mug, add a tiny pinch of salt and stir well. Have your partner taste from each mug and then ask them to rate the drinks from least sweet to most sweet. Ask them if they think any of the three have sugar added.

> **Becky says:** *If your tester cannot tell a difference between the first and third mugs, add a tiny pinch more salt and try again. You want the bitterness to be reduced without the coffee tasting at all salty. (Make sure they don't see you tinker with it.)*

Honey, Rhubarb, and Thyme Jam MAKES ABOUT 1 CUP

Rhubarb is a sour vegetable and not technically a fruit at all, but come early spring those of us in northern climes are so stark raving desperate for fruit, we slap the label on rhubarb and dump a backhoe of sugar onto it to make it palatable. I love rhubarb, but let's be honest: without sugar, no one would go near the stuff. Even the leaves are poisonous. When balanced correctly, however, the sour and sweet elements of a rhubarb jam or pie do not bury each other, they elevate each other, creating an explosion of sensation. You can serve this jam a variety of ways: stirred into yogurt and topped with pistachios, alongside a selection of local fresh cheeses, or with some cold slices of duck breast. It would also make a nice accompaniment to mustard-glazed roasted pork loin.

- 3 cups rhubarb, cut into medium dice (from about 3 stalks)
- ⅓ cup white wine or champagne vinegar
- ¼ cup dark brown sugar
- 2 tablespoons honey
- 1 tablespoon grated fresh ginger
- 1 tablespoon chopped fresh thyme
- 1 cinnamon stick
- 1 teaspoon lemon zest
- ½ teaspoon fine sea salt
- 10 grinds black pepper

1 Put all the ingredients into a saucepan. Bring to a boil, then reduce to a simmer and cook, stirring often, for about 30 minutes, or until thickened. Remove the cinnamon stick, cool the jam completely, transfer to a jar with lid, and refrigerate until ready to serve. The jam will keep for up to 2 weeks in the fridge, 6 months in the freezer, or, if you're a canning type, for much, much longer.

Cacao Nib and Chocolate Chunk Cookies MAKES APPROXIMATELY 3 DOZEN COOKIES

This is a decidedly adult cookie (and one of my absolute favorites ever); the sweetness is balanced perfectly with bitter notes from the chocolate and cacao nibs. A sprinkle of demerara sugar and Maldon sea salt is the perfect sweet-salty crunchy finish. Tip of the chef knife to food writer Lorna Yee for the inspiration.

- 1 cup (2 sticks) unsalted butter, at room temperature
- 1 cup packed dark brown sugar
- ½ cup demerara sugar, plus more for sprinkling
- ¼ cup granulated sugar
- 2 large eggs
- 1 tablespoon vanilla extract
- ½ tablespoon kosher salt

- 1 teaspoon freshly ground cinnamon
- 1 teaspoon baking soda
- 2 cups all-purpose flour
- 1 cup whole wheat pastry flour
- 12 ounces 70 percent bittersweet chocolate, coarsely chopped
- 2 tablespoons cacao nibs
- Maldon salt, for sprinkling

1 Preheat the oven to 350 degrees F.

2 Cream the butter with all three sugars in the bowl of a stand mixer until light and fluffy, about 3 minutes. Add the eggs, vanilla, salt, cinnamon, and baking soda and mix for 30 seconds on low speed. Gradually add in the flours on low speed and then stir in the chopped chocolate and cacao nibs by hand.

3 Scoop out about 1 heaping tablespoon of dough per cookie and arrange on a baking sheet lined with parchment paper, leaving about 2 inches between cookies. (Do not flatten.) Sprinkle with a little demerara and a few crystals of Maldon salt, if desired. Bake for exactly 12 minutes. The cookies may appear underdone or too soft, but they will set up once they cool down. Wait a minute to transfer them from the pan to a cooling rack. Allow to cool completely (if you can wait that long).

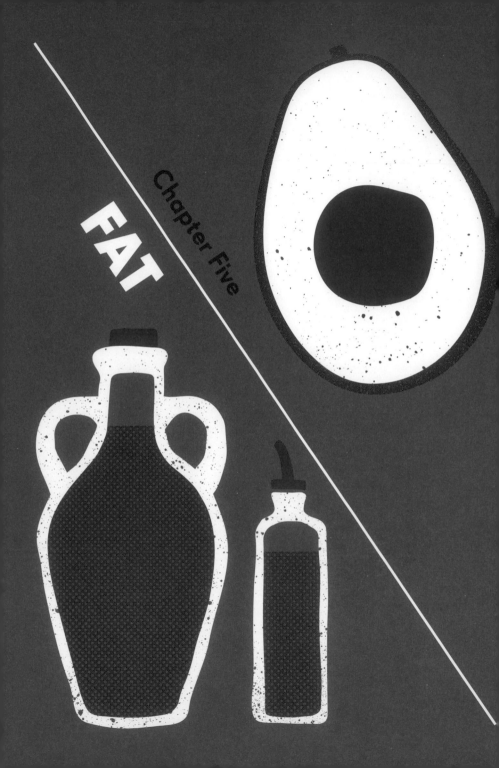

Chapter Five

FAT

The '80s were a bleak time in the American diet—the lean years, quite literally. We avoided fat not because it was expensive and we were poor, but from the mistaken notion that eating fat made us fat.[13] It took us a while to put down our ice milk and come around to the scientific fact that cutting fat out of our diet is deadly at worst and a gross oversimplification of science at best. Fats were replaced with boatloads of sugar: processed food companies got rich, and America got fat. Barbara Moran, writing for *Harvard Public Health* magazine, said of the misleading time, "It was one big, happy, fat-free feeding frenzy—and a public health disaster."

I was a young impressionable teen in those years. I suffered through the confusion and mystery of a "food" product billed as fat-free half-and-half. I'm not sure how "happy" a time it was as we were too tweaked on sugar to take the pulse of our mood. If you were an adult and cooking at home during that decade, I bet you've since dealt with the hassle of trying to offload your fat-free and low-fat cookbooks that no one wants. No one. I'm so glad this dark period in American culinary history is over because if there is one thing we can all agree on now: *fat is fantastic* (and all the SnackWell's Devil's Food Cookie Cakes in the world need to die a fiery death). I exaggerate slightly, but there are hundreds of articles and books about good fats and bad fats and low-fat and no-fat diets, and if you lived through this time you are probably still fighting hard against everything the media told you to fear about fat.

Here's the truth: We are literally hardwired to seek out fat, and it's foolish to fight it. Let go of what we've been told by the proverbial "they." While Americans were drinking blue skim milk and choking down nonfat yogurt, people in Greece were bathing in olive oil and full-fat rich yogurt and living longer than us.[14]

Fat is one of the keys to flavor. It's not that food can't taste good without fat. If you start out with high-quality, seasonal ingredients, use enough salt to amplify their essence, perhaps add a small hit of something acidic or sweet, good things will happen. But with the addition of a bit of fat, we approach greatness. Think of a really good apple, like a Honeycrisp. You bite through the skin (where there is a little natural sodium) and are immediately rewarded with the perfect balance of sweetness and acidity. It's refreshing. It is a really good apple. Do you remember that vintage Reese's commercial where a man eating chocolate bumped into a woman eating peanut butter and created the world's best candy? I wonder if the first person who dipped an apple into caramel felt like a genius. Food can be good—even really, really good—without fat. But great? No dice.

Fat not only makes food great, it even sounds great. Lending weight to how much fat is all about texture, there is a machine that exists in the world called a tribometer that takes quantitative measurements of mouthfeel. It is sometimes made with a pig's tongue. New testing called *acoustic tribology* makes use of a teeny, tiny microphone that goes inside the test subject's mouth, behind their front teeth. It picks up the sound of varying vibrations of papillae (bumps on the tongue) as the tongue rubs against the palate. For example, black coffee alone sounds rougher than coffee with cream, which sounds smooth and velvety. We seek our fat for its dense double hit of calories, but we crave fat for its luscious, velvety texture.

Fat 101

Fat is the newest proposed basic taste, according to recent research.[15] As the lead scientists suggest, you can call it *oleogustus*, which comes from the Latin root "oleo" for oily and "gustus" referring to taste. Or not. Interestingly, the taste of fatty acids alone was not entirely pleasant. Study participants initially reported it as bitter, simply because it was unpleasant, but eventually they were able to determine it was a distinctly different taste than bitter. So maybe isolated fatty acids don't taste great, but butter and burgers sure do.

Besides being a dense source of caloric energy (9 calories per gram compared to 4 calories per gram for carbohydrates and protein), there are seven incredibly important things fat can do for your food:

1   Fat carries flavor by dissolving fat-soluble molecules. So you are quite literally not tasting the whole flavor picture if there is no fat in a dish.

2   Fat contributes to good mouthfeel (one of the more unfortunate words in the English language). It's this textural element of fat that also allows the flavor of food to stick around a little longer. Fat changes the texture of food by creating a satisfying lusciousness. A butter sauce without enough butter swirled in at the end is thin and sharp with acidity; when you've added enough butter, the sauce becomes velvety, rich, and balanced.

3   Fat plays an integral role in an emulsion (a mixture of two or more liquids that are normally not blendable). Without fat, there would be no such thing as mayonnaise, hollandaise, beurre blanc, or ice cream. What a sad world that would be.

4   Fat transmits heat efficiently. A tray of roasted vegetables without it will cook unevenly, in addition to not tasting as great as it would with some duck fat or olive oil. Mmmm, duck fat.

5   Fat prevents food from sticking to the pan. A swirl of fat in the pan makes all the difference between a beautiful seared piece of fish and a stuck-on, broken-up fillet that a cook needs to deploy an arsenal of spatulas and tongs to dislodge. "But I have an entire collection of nonstick pans," you say. In general, I don't recommend nonstick pans because they can't take higher heat and don't sear foods

very well. (I'm also not entirely sure about the black magic that is making them nonstick and it kind of scares me.) I only own one nonstick pan for cooking omelets and crepes, and I'm very careful not to scratch the coating. Seasoned cast-iron is my preferred pan for a million reasons (for more on caring for cast iron, head here: bit.ly/2pyukpp).

6   Fat covers over a world of overcooking. The reason why people are scared to cook fish is that there is a very thin margin for error. A slightly overcooked fatty steak? Under- or overcooked bacon—still really, really good. Fat saves a cook when the heat and time have gotten off track.

7   When it comes to baking, fats can also add air (through creaming with sugar or beating) and "shorten" doughs by hindering the formation of gluten (think of a light, tender pie dough).

Types of Fat

Culinary fats consist of a combination of saturated, polyunsaturated, and monounsaturated fats. For example, extra-virgin olive oil is primarily monounsaturated fat, but 13 percent of it is saturated fat.

Saturated fats are solid at room temperature and somewhat resistant to rancidity. Coconut oil is approximately 90 percent saturated fat, butter is approximately 50 percent saturated fat, and lard is approximately 39 percent saturated fat.

Polyunsaturated fats are liquid at room temperature and highly susceptible to rancidity (safflower and sunflower oils).

Monounsaturated fats are liquid at room temperature and moderately susceptible to rancidity (avocado, canola, olive, and nut oils).

Substituting Fat for Fat

Beef suet and lard can substitute for each other, while duck fat and chicken fat (schmaltz) would offer similar flavor profiles. Nut oils are unique, but if you don't have almond oil, try walnut or hazelnut. Neutral oils such as avocado, peanut, safflower, sunflower, and canola are absolutely interchangeable, as they have little to no flavor. When it comes to replacing the butter in a butter sauce, I haven't found a substitution that is even remotely the same, no matter what you may have read. In a pinch, I've blended a fruity olive oil into a sauce (literally in a blender) to finish it with good, but different, flavor results.

> **(NOT-SO-)FUN FACT** There ain't no such thing as a free lunch. Americans learned this lesson the hard way when olestra, an artificially hydrogenated trans fat, was unleashed on the public. With all the satisfaction of fat on the palate, it nonetheless passed through the body calorie-free. The problem? It passed through the body at a time and speed of its own choosing (and—bonus—took nutrients right along with it). In the late '90s, you ate a whole can of Pringles at your own peril.

Smoke Point

Smoke point is the temperature at which fats begin to smoke and burn. Despite what every badass chef has ever proclaimed on TV, "heat the oil until it smokes" is not recommended, for the sake of the fat, your home insurance deductible, and your health. Once the fat has been heated to its smoke point or beyond, it begins to break down and create so-called free radicals that roam around your body like the Chicago Eight in the '60s, rioting and creating mayhem. Plus it can literally ignite. (The oil, not your body.)

Follow these guidelines to determine the right fat to cook with:

- Use low smoke point and unfiltered fats, including walnut oil and expensive extra-virgin olive oil, for dressings and finishing dishes, and butter for pan sauces, glazing protein as a finishing technique, and eating off of bread (mmm, butter).

- Unrefined flaxseed oil has a smoke point of 225 degrees F, which is very, very low and recommended for creating a glass-like seasoning on cast-iron pans, among other uses.

- Use medium smoke point fats—such as coconut oil, olive oil, and butter cut with a high-heat oil for low- to medium-heat cooking. Note: Despite the lower smoke point of extra-virgin olive oil (325 to 375 degrees F), Daniel Gritzer, culinary director of Serious Eats, could not find any scientific articles clearly supporting the idea that exposing olive oils to high heat has negative health consequences. In fact olive oil, as an exception, seems to hold up well at higher heats.[16]

- Use high smoke point, refined (filtered), or clarified fats, such as ghee or avocado or peanut oil, for frying and searing. Avocado oil has a smoke point of 520 degrees F. Or, as mentioned, skirt commonly circulated, but not scientifically backed-up advice, and use olive oil for all your cooking needs.

Rancidity

A fat becomes rancid when it begins to deteriorate, causing the development of unpleasant musty or waxy odors. I asked a selection of people what rancid fat smelled like to them, and I got answers ranging from "nail polish remover," to "petroleum," to "old candle wax." To me rancid oils smell like old Play-Doh all the way.

Oxygen, light, and heat are the top reasons a fat goes "off." Resist buying the super cheap vats of oil from Costco unless you're planning to deep-fry ten turkeys in one month. I store only a small amount of the oil I need at room temperature, ready to go. The backups go in the cold, dark fridge. Olive oil will solidify when refrigerated. Simply bring the bottle out and let it sit for an hour or so, then decant what you need, when you need it. I also store nuts and seeds in the fridge or freezer, except for small amounts I'll go through quickly.

Once you are familiar with the smell and taste of rancid fats, you will automatically know how to ensure food tastes its best. Few people recognize this off smell and flavor as it progresses or how often it is apparent in your food—especially in specialty oils, like walnut, sesame, or flaxseed; whole grain flours and crackers; and nuts and seeds. I once made a vinaigrette, used it to dress a salad, and took a bite just prior to plating. Man did I regret not smelling my "new" bottle of olive oil before ruining the entire salad with it. Now I obsessively smell a bottle each time I use it to make sure it's still fresh. Keep in mind that there's a progression and a fat doesn't get fully funky until some time has passed. That bad bottle of oil I had? I probably forgot to check the date on it, and/or it was stored improperly by the distributor or grocer, or some combination of these occurred.

If you have no idea what rancidity smells like, create some for yourself by buying a fresh bottle of extra-virgin olive oil. Check the label to make sure the oil was pressed this year, and also to verify it has no added antioxidants that protect against rancidity—such as BHA, BHT, or vitamin E—as the experiment won't work well. Smell the oil initially when you buy it. Try to remember that clean, bright scent. Pour a small amount out in a lidded jar and leave it in a warm, bright place. It will slowly start to break down. Smell it every week. You will soon know exactly what a rancid fat smells like, and while it won't make you sick in an acute way, research suggests it's not good for health in the long term.[17]

Fat-Soluble Molecules

Most flavor molecules are hydrophobic, which sounds like they are scared of water and in truth they are, but what it really means for our purposes is that they are soluble in fat. Putting herbs in a pot of water for stock is a great idea in theory, but adding them directly to water and not to fat means that a lot of the volatile aromatics evaporate into the air; this makes your house smell great but you haven't captured as much flavor as you could. Sauté those herbs with an onion in a bit of oil first and then add the water for the stock? The flavor blooms.

WHEN TO ADD MORE FAT

1 If a dish's acidity is too high and you want to tone it down a bit, particularly when adding something sweet isn't desired or you've already done so and need another tool. Think about how this works in vinaigrettes.
2 If you feel that the flavors of the aromatics aren't coming through, a little more fat can help (but be wary of adding a ton of cream in particular).
3 If you simply want a creamier mouthfeel.

Keeping Fat in Check

Some people think there is no such thing as too much fat. Those same people may also need their gallbladder removed. The overarching theme of this book is balance, so I firmly believe that if you are eating a wide range of dishes and one of them is really fatty, it will all work out—especially if one of the complementary dishes is a bracing pickle or full of absorbing starch. But one dish and one dish only that is covered in grease? Well, there are bad times ahead for your stomach, and you likely won't look back on that meal too favorably. A little fat goes a long way.

If you find that your dish is too fatty, defatting is the best strategy, if possible. The basic method involves chilling to solidify the fat, which naturally rises to the surface. Later, the fat can easily be removed. If there is no time for chilling, simply skim the fat off the surface as you are cooking (see a specific example of defatting on page 80). Alternatively, try adding more acid to cut the perception of fat. Or you could serve the dish with starch to absorb excess fat. Fat is like a blanket on your taste buds. You stay warm and it's cozy and comforting, but you can't feel things as readily. Too much cream or fat in a soup and your tongue transforms into Kenny from *South Park*, his warm coat zipped up around his face, totally cut off from the world. You know what happens to Kenny in every episode? He dies. And he never sees it coming.

Fat coats the tongue and while, yes, it can dissolve fat-soluble molecules, it can also dull the senses a bit. Imagine tasting a soup with lots of herbs, and then imagine adding a cup of cream to it. The texture will change and the soup might be more satisfying, but the direct hit of those herbs will be dulled a bit. That being said, when starting a sauté, you have to use more than 1 teaspoon of oil to contribute flavor to the dish. As such, you should circle the pan with the fat, using at least 1 to 2 tablespoons for most dishes.

FUN FACT Confit—from the French *confire*, meaning "to preserve"—is a traditional Southwestern French cooking method where meat (typically goose or duck legs) is lightly cured for a few days, cooked low and slow in fat, and then stored under the cooling fat. The fat forms a protective barrier, keeping microbes out of the meat, while the meat becomes luscious, sexy, and über-rich. It was all the rage before refrigeration, but we still eat it today because FAT.

Roasted Winter Vegetables with Dates and Prosciutto Vinaigrette MAKES 4 SERVINGS

There's something about this salad that hits all the right cozy winter nesting sweet spots. I love how the sweet, rich dates play with the fatty cured pork. Balsamic vinegar echoes the sweetness while carrying enough acidity to cut the fat of the olive oil and prosciutto. Serve this dish alongside a roasted chicken or on its own topped with a poached egg.

- 1 large unpeeled orange sweet potato, cut into large dice
- 1 large unpeeled delicata squash, halved lengthwise, seeded, and cut crosswise into ½-inch slices
- ½ pound brussels sprouts, ends trimmed, halved lengthwise
- ¼ cup extra-virgin olive oil, divided
- ½ teaspoon fine sea salt
- 5 medjool dates, cut lengthwise into sixths
- 2 ounces prosciutto, cut into small dice
- 1 tablespoon finely diced shallot
- 1 teaspoon lightly crushed fennel seed (optional)
- ¼ teaspoon red pepper flakes
- ⅓ cup unsalted or low-sodium chicken stock
- 2 tablespoons balsamic vinegar
- 1 tablespoon light brown sugar
- 1 teaspoon orange zest

1 Preheat the oven to 450 degrees F.

2 Arrange the sweet potato, squash, and brussels sprouts on a parchment paper–lined baking sheet and drizzle 2 tablespoons of the olive oil over the vegetables. Toss well and then sprinkle evenly with the salt. Flip the cut sides of the vegetables down onto the tray. Don't overcrowd the pan—use two if needed. Roast for 15 minutes, then add the dates, mixing them through. Cook for another 15 to 20 minutes, or until the vegetables are tender throughout and caramelized around the edges.

3 Meanwhile, make the vinaigrette. Heat the remaining 2 tablespoons olive oil in a frying pan over medium heat. Add the prosciutto and slowly render out all the fat until it crisps up.

Remove the prosciutto with a slotted spoon and drain on paper towels, leaving the fat in the pan. Add the shallot, fennel seed, and red pepper flakes to the pan. Once the shallot has softened, about 5 minutes, add the chicken stock, balsamic, and brown sugar. Simmer until the liquid has reduced in volume by one-third. Remove the pan from the heat and pour the vinaigrette into a bowl or jar. Stir three-quarters of the crispy prosciutto back into the vinaigrette, along with the orange zest. You can also blend the vinaigrette with the added prosciutto to create a creamy, thicker dressing. The vinaigrette will keep for up to 1 week in your refrigerator.

4 Drizzle the vinaigrette over the vegetables and toss well. Divide among four plates and top each with a little of the remaining crispy prosciutto bits.

Gummy's Brisket MAKES 10 TO 12 SERVINGS

The acidity in the red wine and mustard are the key to cutting the fat in this recipe, as well as pairing it with potatoes to help soak up some of the richness. This dish was quintessential Friday night dinner fare at my grandmother's house. My grandfather would stand at the head of the table and carve the brisket into thin slices across the grain. I can still see those slices, held together by the thinnest of forces, falling off the edge of his knife as we all watched, our mouths watering. Pass the horseradish.

For the brisket:
- 1 (8- to 10-pound) whole brisket (the fattier "deckle" or second cut on top and the leaner "first" cut underneath separated from each other with a layer of delicious fat; call your butcher to order this)
- 2 teaspoons fine sea salt
- 2 tablespoons high-heat fat, such as ghee, or high-heat oil, such as avocado, divided
- 1 teaspoon freshly ground black pepper
- 5 onions, sliced into ½-inch half-moons
- 4 dried bay leaves
- 1 tablespoon whole grain mustard
- 2 cups full-bodied red wine, such as cabernet sauvignon or Syrah
- 1 cup unsalted beef or chicken stock (or water)
- 16 skin-on small potatoes, such as fingerling or new
- 3 medium carrots, sliced into ½-inch coins
- 2 large stalks celery, sliced ½ inch thick

For the horseradish cream:
- ½ cup heavy whipping cream
- ½ cup mayonnaise
- ½ cup prepared horseradish
- ½ teaspoon honey
- ¼ teaspoon fine sea salt

1 Season the brisket with the salt the day before you plan to cook it and refrigerate overnight, uncovered.

2 When you are ready to proceed with cooking, preheat the oven to 300 degrees F.

3 In a large Dutch oven or cast-iron pot, heat 1 tablespoon of the ghee or avocado oil over high heat. Sprinkle the black pepper over the brisket. Add the brisket to the pot and brown well, turning occasionally, until deeply caramelized on all sides, about 20 minutes total. Remove the brisket from the pot and set aside. Add the remaining 1 tablespoon oil to the pot along with the onions. Cook, stirring frequently, until the onions are lightly browned, 20 to 25 minutes. Return the brisket to the pot, fat side up, on top of the onions, along with the bay leaves. Brush the mustard over the brisket and pour the wine and stock around the sides.

4 Place the pot in the oven, uncovered, and bake for 2½ to 3 hours, turning the brisket over every 45 minutes or so. After 2 hours, tuck the potatoes, carrots, and celery around the brisket and continue braising until the vegetables are tender, about 30 minutes. Lift out the brisket and defat the braising liquid (see Note for the best method). The brisket will keep in an airtight container in the refrigerator for up to 2 days.

5 About 1 hour before serving, preheat the oven to 300 degrees F. Transfer the brisket to a shallow roasting pan or baking dish and spoon the defatted juices and vegetables on top. Cover tightly with foil and bake until heated through, about 45 minutes.

6 Meanwhile, prepare the horseradish cream. Whip the heavy cream in a bowl until soft peaks form. In another bowl, combine the mayonnaise and horseradish. Add the honey and salt to taste and stir well. Gently fold the horseradish mixture into the whipped cream until incorporated. The horseradish cream will keep, covered, in the refrigerator for up to 3 hours. (It will keep for a few days in the fridge, but it will have lost its lightness from the whipped cream.)

7 Transfer the brisket to a cutting board and slice across the grain into ¼-inch-thick slices. Arrange the meat and vegetables on a platter, drizzle with the juices, and serve with the horseradish cream on the side.

Note: *The best way to defat the braising liquid is to make the dish a day ahead. Lift out the meat and strain the hot juices. Store the meat and vegetables in a separate container in the refrigerator. Pour the juices into a tall, narrow container and refrigerate. The next day all the fat will have risen to the top. Remove it (you can reserve these drippings for cooking) and recombine the juices with the meat and vegetables to reheat for serving.*

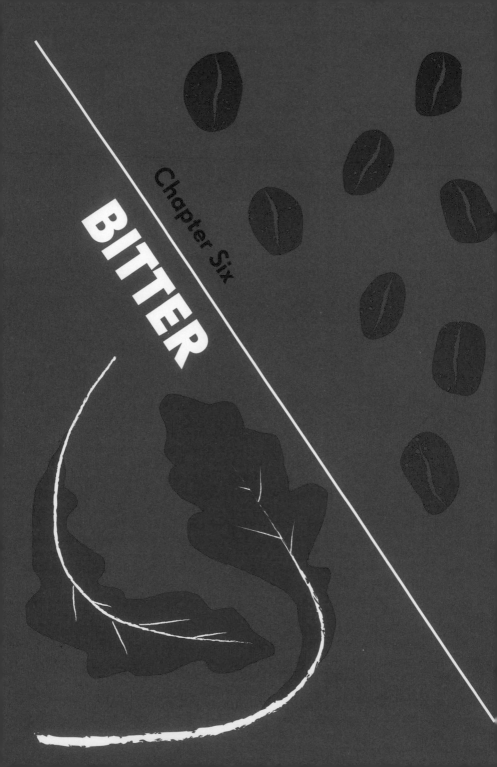

Chapter Six

BITTER

Bitter needs a better PR agent. The word signifies something difficult to swallow, both literally and figuratively. Children can't stand it. A minority of people (likely tolerant tasters) brag about their love of dark roast black coffee, extra-dark chocolate, and super hoppy beers. Some people confuse bitterness with astringency, thinking the drying sensation on their tongue is the same thing as the bitter taste. But the long-lasting puckering and drying sensations are from phenol-rich compounds like tannins. Remember that bitter is a basic taste, not a texture or feeling. We'll get to tannins in Chapter 10, but a triggering of the trigeminal nerve is what is actually responsible for that sensation some confuse with bitterness, possibly because some bitter things are *also* astringent. Other people confuse bitter with sour,[18] but bitter is more tongue-curling, long-lasting, and unpleasant, whereas sour is puckering and mouth-watering. For example, grapefruit is sometimes labeled as bitter, and it's true that there is a bit of bitterness in the fruit, but it's more sour than bitter. Chew on a strip of the peel by itself to really nail down what bitter is. Then rinse your mouth out and taste the flesh, which is sour. Go back and forth to get it down.

In Chapter 4 we learned that children are born with a greater desire for sweetness because sugar is a signifier of calories; children are also extra sensitive to the bitter taste because it's a potential toxin. I didn't know any of this, of course, when I was a kid; I simply knew that a lot of foods tasted yucky and sweet stuff was the best. I also knew something else: coffee, in particular, was a cruel joke played on children. The adults in my life were addicted to the toasty, rich concoction, the smell of which wafted into my bedroom as I woke up. So important was this beverage that it outranked us in the morning. "No questions until we're done with our coffee," we were told. Naturally, my brothers and I had to try this amazing elixir, so powerful it could silence children. That early taste of coffee was not my worst life disappointment, but it might have been one of my first. My tastes have since changed, in part because I've lost bitter receptors with the general loss of taste buds, which happens as we age, but I've also been acted upon by cultural pressures to push myself to get used to more bitter things. You might discover the same change is happening with you as you mature. You can learn to get used to many tastes, no matter your taster status or your age, with repetition and a healthy dose of peer pressure.

BITTER BEFORE AND BITTER AFTER

You may have heard of aperitifs and digestifs and wondered what the heck was the difference. There is much debate, but let me simplify it a bit: low alcohol, dry beverages—such as dry vermouth, champagne, or Campari and soda—are meant to be served before dinner (aperitif), while sweeter, more bitter, boozier options, such as Fernet and other amari, should follow a meal (digestif).

The bitter extraction of herbs, roots, and spices in amari (*amaro* is the Italian word for "bitter," and amari are bittersweet herbal liqueurs) help release saliva, gastric juices, and digestive enzymes. Most people prefer them after their meal, but I like to do both: a little bitter before *and* after. Give it a try. I recommend Campari and soda before dinner (with a splash of sweet vermouth if you need it sweeter), an Aperol spritz, or Lillet, and then Underberg (German), Chartreuse (French), or Averna (Italian) afterward.

If you are one of those people who can't quite put your finger on the differences between bitter, sour, and astringent (tannic), a helpful, though potentially unpleasant, experiment involves looking in a mirror while you sample the following items in progression, rinsing your mouth between each one. First suck a lemon, then swallow a few dashes of bitters, and finish by sucking on a used black tea bag. Better yet, have a friend record you doing it and then send the footage to me as soon as you possibly can, because the hope that this might happen is what I am now living for.

FUN FACT It's clearly evolutionarily protective to detect bitterness, so much so that humans have about two dozen or more types of bitter receptors yet only a few sweet ones. Jellyfish, fruit flies, and bacteria can all sense bitter compounds too.

Bitter 101

Bitterness pulls your mind into sharp focus; as your taste receptors fire, you ask yourself what is causing the minor or major assault on your palate and you make a split-second decision about whether you're going to swallow or not. This sensation, when not overdone, likely recalls our hardwired aversion to the toxins often associated with bitter flavors. Sweet soothes the palate; bitter jars it, shakes it, brings it into sharp relief. Just like some can be addicted to sweet or fatty foods, some are drawn to this sharp and sophisticated component of taste. Bitter is a knife slicing through butter, cutting the palate-coating richness, suppressing sweetness in its path and leaving complexity in its wake.

Allow me to introduce you to the diverse family of bitters, which includes members of the vegetable, spice, and fruit worlds: citrus zest; the caffeine in chocolate, tea, and coffee; hops; brassicas like brussels sprouts, kale, rapini, turnips, arugula, and horseradish; bitter melon; fenugreek; celery leaves; walnuts; charred foods like caramel and burnt toast; and many, many more.

FUN FACT Ever wonder why orange juice tastes terribly bitter after you've brushed your teeth? You might think it's because mint and orange don't go well together but it's not that (mint and citrus make a fine salad). The reason stems from two compounds added to most toothpastes: sodium lauryl sulfate and sodium lauryl ether sulfate.[19] Both compounds suppress our sweet taste receptors and make our bitter taste receptors more sensitive. Voilà: bitter and foul OJ. Turns out these compounds are in toothpaste for their "tingle" factor and not the health of our teeth, so you can look for brands without them or brush your teeth after breakfast.

Keeping Bitter in Line

Even with the added complexity bitterness brings to food, for most people it's something to be managed versus encouraged. As covered in Chapter 2, salt is the best way to deemphasize bitterness and bring forward other tastes, but there are other tools in your bag in case you have already added enough salt and still find the level of bitterness in the dish out of whack.

- **Caramelizing:** For many vegetables, roasting, searing, or braising can reduce bitterness by bringing out natural sweetness and helping bitter juices evaporate off. Note that there are a few exceptions to this—for instance, arugula can become more bitter when cooked.
- **Blanching:** While I tend to use this method a bit less because it also robs some of the nutrition, dunking brussels sprouts,

rapini, or kale in boiling salted water for a minute or two and then shocking it in ice water to halt cooking can mitigate some of the bitterness.

- **Rinsing:** When kale is chopped, an enzyme (myrosinase) and sulfur-containing components (glucosinolates) combine to create a bitter hell-child known as isothiocyanates. A quick rinse after chopping or massaging kale will remove some of this bitterness.

- **Sweetening:** Adding a sweet element to the dish, such as honey or raisins, will result in what's known as *mutual suppression*. In other words, the bitter will be turned down by the sweet and the sweet will be turned down by the bitter.

- **Diluting:** Bulking up a dish is an effective way to spread out the bitterness a little. Bitter can add complexity but a little goes a long way. Using blander ingredients such as beans or croutons allows the positive aspects of bitterness to shine through without overwhelming the palate. (See the recipe for Warm Radicchio Salad with White Beans and Smoked Sea Salt on page 90 for an example of this.)

- **Fattening:** Because fat coats the tongue, it helps to mask bitterness. Think tossing brussels sprouts with olive oil or adding cream to coffee.

- **Warming:** Warm or hot foods mask bitter tastes better than cold. That cup of coffee will always taste less bitter while piping hot than half an hour later. The hotter or colder a food, the less your taste buds are able to detect anything. (Read more about manipulating the temperature of foods to achieve your desired results in Chapter 11.)

FUN FACT Sensitive tasters (25 percent of the population) tend to prefer more salt in their food because they experience bitterness more intensely than average or tolerant tasters. Whether they are aware of it or not, they reach for salt because it makes their food more palatable.

Experiment Time

Lesson: Show the magic powers of salt to turn down bitterness.

Materials needed: Fine sea salt, 1 unpeeled regular cucumber, 8 ounces strong brewed dark-roast coffee, 1 bottle of super hoppy IPA.

Cucumber

Slice the cucumber (not an English cucumber) into ¼-inch rounds. Eat one slice. Note what you taste. Is it sweet? Slightly bitter at the finish? Sprinkle a few grains of fine sea salt on another slice and let it sit for 2 to 3 minutes to allow it to absorb a bit. Now taste the salted cucumber. Do you notice an increase in sweetness and a decrease in bitterness?

Coffee

Brew or purchase a cup of strong coffee. If you buy it, get an Americano from Starbucks; their coffee is roasted very dark (some might say burnt) and has a distinct bitterness. Divide the coffee between two cups. In one, put a tiny pinch of fine sea salt and stir well. Leave the other as is. Taste and compare. If you don't detect a noticeable difference, keep adding tiny bits of salt to the first cup until you can. The salted coffee should not taste salty at all, but you should notice a distinct lessening of the bitterness. Personally, I think salting coffee works more efficiently than sweetener. You can also play around with using a combination of a little salt and a little sweetener to your taste.

IPA

Recreate the same exact experiment with IPA as you did with the coffee (minus any sweetener).

> **FUN FACT** Most people think that coffee is inherently bitter, but author and food developer Barb Stuckey knows

the truth. In fact, only 10 percent of bitterness in coffee is from the caffeine. The rest of it comes from phenolic acids that are a result of the roasting and brewing processes. The darker the roast, the more bitter the brew.

Experiment Time

Lesson: Show how bitterness balances cloying sweetness and creates depth and complexity.

Classic Manhattan MAKES 2 COCKTAILS

- 2 ounces rye whiskey or bourbon (rye is traditional, but bourbon is lovely)
- 1 ounce sweet red vermouth (I prefer Antica Formula)

- Maraschino cherries, for garnish (Luxardo is the best)
- 4 dashes Angostura or orange bitters (there are a world of choices here, though, so go with any favorite!), divided

1 This experiment is painfully easy. Add the whiskey and vermouth to a glass or jar and fill with ice. Stir well. Strain into two chilled martini glasses. Add a cherry to each glass. Add 2 dashes of the bitters to the second glass and stir gently but thoroughly. Taste the first Manhattan without bitters. Rinse your mouth with water. Then taste the second. The first drink will be boozy, sort of one-dimensional, tilting toward cloying. The second, with the addition of the bitters, should be more balanced, complex, and well rounded. Now add the remaining 2 dashes bitters to the first drink, because learning time is over and there's no excuse for a bad drink.

Warm Radicchio Salad with White Beans and Smoked Sea Salt MAKES 4 SERVINGS

Four bitterness-balancing methods discussed in this chapter are used in this recipe: Dilution by having the bitter radicchio comprise only a small part of the finished dish. Caramelization of the radicchio to increase its natural sweetness. Salting to turn down the perception of bitterness. And finally, sweetness in the form of honey for balance.

- 1 cup dried cannellini beans, or 2 (14-ounce) cans cannellini beans, rinsed and drained
- 1 tablespoon kosher salt
- 1 tablespoon extra-virgin olive oil
- ¼ cup chopped shallot
- 1 head radicchio, cored and cut into bite-size pieces
- 1 teaspoon honey
- ½ teaspoon finely chopped fresh rosemary
- Smoked sea salt
- 1 cup croutons (bread cubed and dried in a 300-degree-F oven for 15 minutes)
- 1 cup Italian Salsa Verde (page 45)

1 If using dried beans, soak them in 1 quart water with the kosher salt and refrigerate overnight. Drain the beans, transfer to a medium pot, cover with fresh water by at least 3 inches, and add a pinch of salt. Bring to a boil and simmer over medium-low heat for 45 to 60 minutes, or until the beans are tender. Set aside to cool in the cooking liquid.

2 Meanwhile, heat the olive oil in a medium sauté pan over medium-high heat. Add the shallot and cook for 5 minutes, or until tender. Add the radicchio, honey, rosemary, and smoked sea salt to taste, and cook until the radicchio starts to lightly brown around the edges, 5 to 7 minutes.

3 Drain the beans and add them to a large bowl along with the radicchio mixture and croutons. Dress with half of the salsa verde and toss gently to incorporate. Taste and add more salsa verde if desired.

Coffee and Chocolate–Braised Short Ribs MAKES 6 TO 8 SERVINGS

Dark roast coffee and dark chocolate are both bitter elements that break up the fattiness of the short ribs, adding complexity and depth to this rich, savory recipe. Brown sugar and bell pepper offer a sweet assist.

- 5 pounds beef short ribs
- 1 tablespoon fine sea salt
- 3 tablespoons brown sugar
- 1½ tablespoons ancho chile powder, plus more to taste
- 1 tablespoon roasted coffee beans
- 2 teaspoons cumin seeds
- 2 teaspoons dried oregano
- 2 tablespoons high-heat oil, such as avocado
- 1 large onion, cut into medium dice
- 1 large red bell pepper, cut into medium dice
- 2 serrano chiles, charred, and then minced (seeds and membranes left in)
- 3 cloves garlic, minced
- 2 cups strong brewed dark roast coffee
- 1 (28-ounce) can fire-roasted whole tomatoes (I prefer Muir Glen)
- 1 tablespoon tomato paste
- ½ cup roughly chopped 70 percent dark chocolate
- 1 cup chopped cilantro, for garnish
- 4 cups Creamy Polenta (recipe follows)

1 Ideally 6 to 8 hours in advance but at the very least 2 hours ahead of cooking, salt the short ribs and refrigerate them.
2 When you are ready to proceed with cooking, preheat the oven to 300 degrees F.
3 Grind the brown sugar, ancho chile powder, coffee beans, cumin, and oregano in a spice grinder until powdered. Set aside.
4 Place the oil in a heavy-bottomed pot over medium-high heat. Working in batches, sear the short ribs until nicely browned. Transfer to a platter and set aside.
5 Reduce the heat to medium and add the onion, bell pepper, and chiles to the pot, stirring until the onions are translucent. Add

the garlic and ground spice mixture, stirring well to incorporate, and cook for 5 minutes. Stir in the coffee, whole tomatoes, and tomato paste and bring the mixture to a boil. Add the short ribs and any collected juices to the pot and return to a boil.

6 Transfer the pot to the oven and bake, uncovered, until the beef is very tender, 3 to 4 hours, turning the ribs over in the sauce every hour. Once the beef is fork-tender, skim the fat off the top. Stir in the chocolate until melted and evenly distributed in the sauce. Season to taste with salt and extra ancho chile powder, if desired. Garnish with cilantro and serve with the polenta.

Creamy Polenta MAKES 4 SERVINGS

- 4 cups unsalted vegetable broth
- 1 teaspoon fine sea salt (omit if using salted broth)
- 1 cup polenta (corn grits)
- 2 tablespoons unsalted butter

1 In a large saucepan over high heat, bring the broth and salt to a rolling boil. Reduce the heat to medium and add the polenta slowly, whisking constantly to avoid lumps. Cook gently over low heat for 20 minutes, stirring frequently until the polenta is thick and creamy. Add the butter and stir to thoroughly incorporate. Season to taste and serve immediately.

Chapter Seven

UMAMI

醤油

Conjure up the food you crave. What gets you into your car, out on a city street, or on your phone paying delivery apps a ransom? In America it's most likely hamburgers, BBQ, sushi, pizza, or anything with bacon or french fries. All of these savory craveables are high in umami—the buzzword that everyone is talking about but few know what the hell it means. UrbanDictionary.com, where I go when I want to understand the slang "those crazy kids" are using these days, had this to say about umami:

> "A bullshit [invented] flavor that TV chefs pretend to be able to recognize but can never define. Due to peer pressure they regurgitate keywords to make it appear that they know what it is, but in reality none of them have a clue."
>
> "Dude I just saw Andrew Zimmern describe some butter as having an umami flavor. Last episode it was mushrooms. I'm pretty sure they are making this shit up as they go."

There's a sliver of truth in the first "definition": a lot of people are confused about what umami is. The second entry, while funny, is untrue, as mushrooms are super high in umami.

Umami 101

Umami is a taste resulting from multiple receptors sensitive to amino acids (mainly glutamate) and nucleotides (mainly guanosine [GMP] and inosine [IMP]) that, together, give food a supercharged "savory" sensation. Clear as mud, right? Less technically, umami is the savoriness, depth, and deliciousness in food that is protein-rich, cured, fermented, fungal, or from the sea (seaweed and shellfish). The breakdown of proteins into glutamate and other amino acids leads to the savory taste that is umami. Rowan Jacobsen, author of many fantastic books including *Apples* and *The Essential Oyster*, points out that "a not insignificant amount of the world's culinary heritage is devoted to ways of doing precisely that [protein breakdown]. Fermentation does it, when bacteria attack the protein. Smoking and curing and dry-aging do it. Microbes break down milk protein during cheesemaking. And, of course, intense or prolonged heat does it, as in grilling or roasting."

There are six ways that Nacho Cheese flavored Doritos hook you with umami. Three are in whole foods form: Romano cheese, cheddar cheese, and tomato powder. The other three are in targeted weapons-grade form: MSG (more on this on page 102) and free nucleotides IMP and GMP, all of which supercharge the umami hit.

If you've smacked your lips and been generally delighted by what you are eating, my guess is that it's probably something rich in umami. I asked my food friends to describe what umami tastes like, without using an ingredient as a crutch. "It's like a party in my mouth," said Matthew. "It's the essence of beefiness," said Michelle. "When something is full of umami, I taste it in the back corners of my mouth." Umami is brothy, savory, round, rich, mouth-filling, and meaty. The word itself is borrowed from the Japanese language: umami or うま味 can be broken apart into うまい or "umai," which means "delicious," and 味 or "mi" which translates to "taste."

When you eat something that's full of umami, your salivary glands kick into high gear and all parts of your mouth respond (the roof, back of the mouth, throat—you may even feel a grippy, coating sensation on the tongue). After you've swallowed, the savory, satisfying aftertaste lasts. It sounds dramatic but it's actually fairly subtle when you eat umami-rich whole foods. On the processed side of the fence, it's a little less subtle: Doritos, for example, are a perfectly engineered food product, precisely injected with umami (MSG) and perfectly balanced amounts of salt, acidity, sugar, and fat. Add a satisfying texture and sound, and try to find your "off" switch.[20]

NATURAL FLAVOR ENHANCERS

Without knowing the scientific basis of the umami taste, cooks have been using the following ingredients to enhance their food for centuries:

- Mushrooms, especially dried shiitake mushrooms
- Sun-dried tomatoes, tomato paste, and ketchup
- Parmesan and blue cheeses
- Anchovies and fish sauce
- Soy sauce
- Vegemite and Marmite
- Miso
- Cured meats
- Nutritional yeast
- Fermented fish
- Carrots
- Potatoes
- Cabbage
- Spinach
- Celery
- Green tea
- Seaweed, especially kombu
- Shellfish, especially clams and shrimp paste

Umami Origin Story

In 2009, a scientific review confirmed that we have receptors specific to glutamate, and therefore, umami should be considered the fifth recognized basic taste, joining salt, sweet, bitter, and sour. Upon hearing the news, Japan was like, "Hi, glad you finally joined us—we've built our entire cuisine around umami." Meet the actual discoverer of umami, Dr. Kikunae Ikeda, or Dr. Tasty, as I call him. In 1908, Ikeda determined that glutamate is what makes the taste of kombu seaweed (and its broth) distinct from the other tastes. He called it umami and the Ajinomoto Company went on to manufacture MSG (monosodium glutamate). In the '50s, another scientist, Dr. Akira Kuninaka, brought to light the synergistic relationship between ingredients high in glutamates with ingredients high in GMP and IMP.

Umami and Ingredient Synergy

In keeping with the original ingredients that led to developments in umami research, let's discuss *dashi*, the soup stock at the core of Japanese cuisine. Dashi is made with kombu, which is rich in glutamate, and dried, smoked bonito (tuna) flakes, which are rich in IMP. Dashi is a simple stock to prepare (see page 108 for a recipe) and it makes all that it comes into contact with better, richer, and fuller. The intensity of umami from this synergistic pairing is a powerful culinary tool to have at your disposal. Vegetarians can use dried shiitake, which is rich in GMP, in place of the bonito for a similar, if not identical, result. Examples of similar synergistic pairings include:

- Cabbage and chicken in a soup
- Parmigiano-Reggiano cheese with tomato sauce and mushrooms
- Anchovies and Parmigiano-Reggiano in a Caesar salad
- The cheese and meat in a cheeseburger

Tomatoes, all on their lonesome, are umami overachievers. Hidden in the jelly that holds the seeds of the tomato are both amino acids and nucleotides. Heston Blumenthal, the famous chef-owner of the Fat Duck near London, can be thanked for this knowledge. He noticed the deep umami flavor in the jelly and worked with scientists to prove it. Research came back finding that the jelly was four times higher in umami than the flesh. Tasting panels also rated the jelly higher in perceived acidity and saltiness. Since learning that, I've never again composted the seeds and jelly of a tomato as I was taught to do in culinary school.

DRUNKEN MADMAN PANCAKE

Okonomiyaki (which translates to "cooked how you like it") is an umami powerhouse dish and it may also be something you've never heard of or tasted. Yet.

It's a savory "pancake" of sorts, with ingredients pulled seemingly at random from the mind of a drunken madman, and it epitomizes Japan's obsession with savory flavors. What follows is the basic preparation; every okonomiyaki ingredient that is high in umami is noted in bold. First, you mix **cabbage** with a type of **potato** called *nagaimo* (mountain potato). Next, you stir in green onions, beaten egg, pickled ginger, fried tempura crispy bits (*tenkasu*), salt, **dashi** (kelp/bonito stock), and perhaps some seafood like **shrimp** or **squid** or **scallop**. Then you cook the pancake, topping it with some **pork belly strips**. After flipping it over to cook a bit longer, you drizzle on some **okonomiyaki sauce** (made with **ketchup**, **soy**, and **anchovies**) and then serve the pancake with drizzled mayo, **seaweed flakes**, and **bonito flakes**.

FUN FACT It's likely that your very first drink was bursting with umami. I'm not talking about that regrettable shot of tequila. I'm literally talking about your first drink. Breast milk is approximately as umami-rich as broth. Thanks, Mom!

When to Add Umami to a Dish

1   You've solved for salt, acid, sweet, bitter, and fat but you still wish there was some more oomph in the dish. If you can't afford to add more salt to the dish without making it too salty, lean heavily on umami ingredients that are not cured or preserved (and therefore salty), such as tomato paste or shiitake mushrooms.

2   You feel that the texture is thin and you want to enhance the food's mouthfeel.

3   Someone you are cooking for is on a low-salt diet; umami helps food taste saltier, while adding less sodium overall. Again, be sure to focus on umami-rich ingredients that are not salty, such as tomatoes and dried shiitake mushrooms.

4   You want to make vegetarian food more meaty. Grab mushrooms, aged cheeses, tomatoes, soy sauce, miso, and/or seaweed and go to town.

5   The ingredients you are using are not as flavorful as you'd prefer, and you want to boost the palatability of the food.

Umami seems quite magical, and once people latch on to all that it adds to food, the only thing to keep track of is a budding addiction (first sign: using fish sauce as cologne). Studies have shown that when umami is added to soups, low-salt versions are more palatable than without. Tasters also rated the low-salt versions closer to their ideal salt level when umami was added.[21] Umami can even make you feel more satisfied when you eat, beyond the savoriness factor alone. Studies show that hunger can initially be stimulated by umami-rich foods, but then satiety was increased, meaning that people were satisfied and full faster than when testers ate meals without umami. This gives credence to the notion that umami might be helpful in appetite control.[22] Some of this is common sense—if you're satisfied with what you're eating, you're less likely to quickly crave something else.

A Few Key Umami-Rich Ingredients

1 **Fish sauce:** It can (and should!) be used in all types of cuisines, not just Asian cuisine. Use a splash in soups, sauces, and dressings—or if you're me, put it in everything, all the time. Don't use so much that your food tastes like anchovies, but add enough to create texture and depth. Or use fish sauce in its semi-original form, which is as a salted anchovy; you can melt one into olive oil to start pasta sauces that blow people away with their savoriness. I love fish sauce so much I even wrote a dorky poem about it (see page 103).

2 **Parmigiano-Reggiano:** Grate the cheese over anything and everything. Add the rind to soups, stews, and bean dishes to introduce depth. When the food is done cooking, fish the rind out, turn your back to any people in the room, and use your teeth to scrape off the newly liberated molten cheese layer.

3 **Tomato paste:** Add a tablespoon to a tray of roasting vegetables, to sautéing onions when making a soup or sauce, and to pâtés and dips.

4 **Mushrooms:** Dried shiitakes are an especially versatile source of umami to have in your pantry. Add to vegetable broths, soups, and stir-fries to bump up the savoriness. Or make porcini powder: simply grind dried porcinis into a very fine powder in a spice grinder and mix into sautéing onions or coat a steak with it.

5 **MSG:** Wait, what? Are you scandalized? Read on.

The DL on MSG

MSG, or monosodium glutamate, is a food additive and flavor enhancer that is made via bacterial fermentation, similar to how one makes yogurt or cheese. It has gotten a bad rap because some people claim to have experienced allergic reactions after consuming it, but as with any refined food additive, such as sugar, moderation is key. In actuality, MSG is as unnatural as refined granulated sugar, meaning that you are as unlikely to walk through the woods and fall into a pile of it as you are to stumble into a pile of sugar. Certainly neither are health foods—and I personally prefer to use whole foods to get umami from the source rather than resorting to an additive—but the science is pretty clear: double-blind, placebo-controlled studies with participants who self-reported side effects from MSG showed that MSG had no such ill effects nor that it is unhealthful to humans in reasonable amounts.[23, 24] (To be extra clear, I don't dispute that a reaction is possible, but the science doesn't point to MSG being the culprit. Given this data, we're left to conclude that some other component may be causing the side effects, not the MSG itself.) Regardless, while I occasionally eat Doritos or consume MSG in other processed foods—where forms of it go rogue under other names such as: autolyzed yeast, yeast extract, or anything "hydrolyzed"—it's still preferable to get umami naturally from meat, mushrooms, and cheese (just as I prefer cooking with sugar in the form of fruit or honey). So feel free to hate on MSG, but at least be consistent in also hating on the sugar in your pastry or that morning cup of coffee.

AN ODE TO FISH SAUCE

You tried to break up with me that day.
You spilled in my Toyota.
Perhaps you were ending it all; our world might not be good enough for you.
Your flavor, after all, cannot be contained by this mortal coil.
Your thirst for adventure strained my marriage,
Because as sure as the sun will rise, your scent will linger.
You tried to break up with me that day.
You spilled in my Toyota.
You underestimate yourself.
I kept you.
I burned the Toyota.

Balancing Umami

For a long time I thought you couldn't overdo savoriness in food, but I've recently come to appreciate that even umami can be overdone. You know you have an umami problem when food tastes boring to you if it's not Doritos, cheeseburgers with mushrooms and ketchup, and pizza with all the meats.

So what does too much umami taste like? I needed to know. I roped my friend Kim into an impromptu home experiment. I made dashi (see the recipe on page 108). Even though dashi was where the science of umami began, the taste of dashi is subtle and hard to qualify precisely, so we added MSG (in the form of Ac'cent Flavor Enhancer) to it in incremental amounts and tasted at each stage to see how the glutamate would progressively change the way the dashi tasted. We kept 1 cup of MSG-free dashi separate so we'd have a control to keep going back to if we needed to compare and contrast. We discovered that as we added more MSG, the dashi got more savory and delicious up to a point and then, when we had gone too far, it felt like our cheeks were sucking inward and our tongues were roughed up and twisty. It was not pleasant, but it also wasn't as bad as something that is too salty or too bitter. It felt like my mouth was getting assaulted by too much sensation and it was a touch overwhelming.

We also just tried MSG straight, right from the container, and what follows are our extensive tasting notes:

> *Um, weird, like our tongues are being sucked on by unseen forces. Not totally unpleasant but not good either.*

So we surmised from our experiment and our collective culinary experience that you probably won't suffer umami overdoses unless you're using MSG in your cooking, or perhaps if you're binge-eating vending machine snacks (no judgment here). But if you do find yourself with a dish that tastes too savory, add bulk with more neutral, less savory ingredients to rebalance and reconfigure its focus.

Experiment Time

Lesson: How umami can create depth, texture, and roundness.

There are not too many dishes that can be fixed if you forget to add salt to them, but pureeing the soup in the final stages along with some salt brings it all back together. Fish sauce is the key ingredient in this recipe, both for its salt and, more appropriately to this chapter, its umami and how it creates a round, savory flavor (where prior to adding it, the soup is thin and almost too aromatic). When fish sauce is deployed correctly, you won't taste it but you'll absolutely appreciate its contribution.

Sweet Potato Soup with Chile and Lemongrass MAKES 4 SERVINGS

- 2 tablespoons virgin coconut oil or neutral oil (such as avocado)
- 1 onion, cut into small dice
- 2-inch piece fresh ginger, grated (if organic, no need to peel the skin)
- ½ cup dry white wine or dry white vermouth
- 2 stalks lemongrass, bottom two-thirds only, trimmed and smashed with the side of a knife
- 2 serrano chiles, halved lengthwise, stem and seeds intact
- 3 lime leaves, smacked with your hand to release aromatics
- 3 slices fresh or rehydrated galangal
- 5 cups peeled orange sweet potato, cut into large dice
- 1 quart water or unsalted vegetable broth (it must be unsalted for this experiment)
- Juice of 1 lime, plus more to taste
- 1 teaspoon fine sea salt
- 1 tablespoon fish sauce (I prefer Red Boat brand), plus more if needed
- Honey (optional)
- ¼ cup toasted pumpkin seeds, for garnish

1 Heat the oil in a soup pot over medium-high heat. Add the onion and sauté for 5 minutes, or until it starts to soften.

Becky says: *This is the point where you'd normally add salt, but we're going to hold back on that for the sake of the experiment.*

2 Add the ginger and sauté for a few more minutes. Deglaze with the wine and cook until the wine is gone. Meanwhile, in a piece of cheesecloth, combine the lemongrass, serranos, lime leaves, and galangal. Wrap them up and tie with a knot.

3 Add the sweet potatoes and cheesecloth bag to the pot and stir well for 2 to 3 minutes. Add the water and bring to a boil. Reduce the heat to maintain a simmer, cover with the lid slightly ajar, and cook for 30 minutes, or until the sweet potatoes are soft.

4 When the sweet potatoes are soft, remove the cheesecloth bag and squeeze it with a spoon against the pot to release all the juices. In a blender (or with an immersion blender), puree the soup until smooth, then return it to the pot. Add the lime juice and taste the soup. What do you feel is missing?

●〜〜〜➤

Becky says: *What you might notice is that the bright notes of the lemongrass and lime overwhelm the balance a little, bringing this soup too far into the atmosphere. The lack of salt may be apparent through an emptiness detected mid-palate. The texture of the soup will seem a bit thin and watery.*

5 Now add the sea salt and taste again, writing down your thoughts about whether anything has changed. Then add the fish sauce, taste, and jot down your impressions. Concentrate on how all parts of your tongue feel.

Becky says: *The tone of the soup should have come down to earth a little—and it needed to! It was too bright, too acidic; it had little body, no soul, no depth. Umami from the fish sauce helped round out the flavor. You might feel this as a full-mouth sensation. The texture of the soup will have changed as well. It should feel thicker, even though you added a small amount of a liquid. More of your taste receptors are firing, and the flavor is being held on your tongue, no longer watery in texture. If you're not sensing these things and the soup does not taste salty to you, go ahead and add a bit more fish sauce until you detect these positive changes.*

6 All that is left to do now is determine if you want a bit more sweetness; if so, add the honey. Divide the soup among four bowls, garnish with the pumpkin seeds, and serve.

Pasta alla Speranza

This is a slight twist on my friend John Speranza's take on a classic dish called Pasta alla Gricia and is a study in Italian-style umami-rich cooking that features cured pork and two aged cheeses. John prefers easily accessible pancetta to traditional *guanciale* (pork jowl) and uses both pecorino Romano and Parmigiano-Reggiano as well as a truckload of freshly cracked black pepper (use half the recommended amount if you're wimpy or a sensitive taster). The trick to perfecting this recipe is to use some of the starchy pasta cooking water and vigorously mix the pasta with it and the cheese to form a perfectly emulsified sauce. Enjoy what some would call "adult" mac and cheese.

- 1 tablespoon kosher salt
- 1½ pounds pancetta in a thick chunk, or 1 pound *guanciale* (as it's quite fatty)
- ¼ cup freshly cracked black pepper (a spice grinder makes quick work of this)
- 2 pounds dried bucatini or spaghetti
- Scant cup finely grated pecorino Romano
- ¼ cup finely grated Parmigiano-Reggiano

1 Bring a large pot of water to a boil. Add the kosher salt.
2 Meanwhile, cut the pancetta into lardons (¼ inch by ¼ inch by 1 inch) and place them in a large sauté pan over medium heat. Render the fat out of the pancetta and cook, stirring occasionally, until the lardons turn golden-brown and the fat has become translucent, about 15 minutes. Remove the pan from the heat, add the black pepper, and let the pancetta sit undisturbed.
3 Cook the pasta until al dente and then carefully transfer it to the sauté pan along with 1 cup of the cooking water. Sprinkle the cheese evenly over the pasta and vigorously mix with tongs until there is a nice coating of cheesy, peppery, porky sauce cloaking the pasta. Serve immediately.

Dashi MAKES A SCANT QUART

Dashi is where the science of umami began, and it's the foundational stock at the center of numerous Japanese dishes. You can save the kombu and katsuobushi in a ziplock bag in the freezer to make what's known as second dashi. First dashi is used for its intense umami in sauces, dressings, and miso soup. Second dashi is typically used in meat and vegetable stews where those ingredients will help add additional umami.

- 10 grams kombu (kelp)
- 1 quart water
- 20 grams katsuobushi (dried bonito flakes)

1 Soak the kombu in the water for at least 30 minutes, or overnight in the fridge to get ahead of the game. In a medium saucepan over medium-low heat, bring the kombu and water slowly to a boil; it should take about 10 minutes to see bubbles developing.
2 When it starts to simmer, remove the kombu with tongs. Add the katsuobushi to the water, simmer gently for a few minutes, turn off the heat, and let it cool. When the flakes have settled to the bottom of the pot, strain the dashi through fine-mesh sieve.

Note: *Vegetarians can make a shiitake-kombu dashi by simply using 15 grams dried shiitake mushrooms in place of the katsuobushi. Soak the mushrooms along with the kombu overnight and proceed with the recipe, removing the kombu when it comes to a simmer and continuing to simmer the mushrooms in the dashi for another 10 minutes. Strain before use.*

Chapter Eight

AROMATICS

We're deep into this book and just now talking about herbs and spices. What gives? You wouldn't be alone in thinking that these aromatics are *crucial* in making food endlessly interesting. And I agree with this sentiment in the abstract, but practically speaking I want to remind you that very rarely has someone tasted a bite of something they've made or ordered and said, "It's really good but it's lacking in cumin or tarragon or fenugreek." Possibly Indian food, but it's much more common to find a dish too salty, in need of a squeeze of lemon or dash of vinegar, lacking in sweetness, or begging for a little fat or less bitterness. Herbs and spices inhabit a world of flavor possibilities but are indispensable in your hands only *after* you've mastered salt, acid, sweet, fat, bitter, and umami. Aromatics make good food great—and many cuisines would be unrecognizable from another without them—but in an inexperienced person's hands, aromatics can and often do unleash Pandora's box.

Aromatics 101

Aromatics encompass everything from oranges to caraway to basil to wine. Anything that adds or boosts a dish's flavor can be broadly considered an aromatic. The aromatic quality of alliums and ginger (as well as turmeric and galangal) are legendary, but these important ingredients cross over into many of the elements of taste and flavor covered in other chapters. Onions, when caramelized, can add sweetness to dishes. Garlic, when cooked too quickly and beginning to burn, can add unintended bitterness to a dish. But in discussions of balance, onions and garlic (especially in their raw or lightly cooked form) are notable for how they grab our palate with their sharpness and spiciness. We'll cover them in depth in Chapter 9. For our purposes here, we will focus primarily on aromatic herbs and spices, though toasted nuts, tea, coffee, and smoke are other examples of culinary aromatics.

When we talk about herbs and spices, what parts of a plant are we referring to? Herbs are plant leaves that are fresh or dried. Spices are sourced from a plant's bark, root, and seed. Grasses can also be used in cooking, the most well known of which is lemongrass. Flowers are also delicious and used in cooking. Saffron is a prime example: it comes from the stigma (female reproductive part) of the crocus flower (isn't it amazing to ponder the lengths we go to, and the money we spend, harvesting and drying flower genitalia to put only a teeny-tiny amount in our food?). In the simplest possible terms: aromatics are ingredients that are used in relatively small quantities primarily for their distinctive flavor and/or aroma.

Categorizing Aromatics

You've heard of synesthesia, yes? Where stimulation of one sense leads to an involuntary experience of another, such as people who "see" sounds in color? I'm not claiming that all chefs are synesthetes, but it's not uncommon to hear food professionals discuss ingredients or flavor in terms of "tone" or "notes." When I use the word tone, I mean how low or high the sound of that ingredient is in my mind, and the general quality of the sound. When I cook with cumin, I hear the growly sound of a tuba or bassoon hitting a low note. When I use coriander, a spice that can be both earthy and citrusy, I think of it making a sound like the strum of an acoustic guitar, neither high nor low. When I zest orange peel into a dish, I hear a striker hitting a triangle: *ting*!

LOW TONE
Rumbling, deep, earthy, smoky, warming
Tuba or bassoon
Cinnamon, cloves, cumin, nutmeg, turmeric, oregano, paprika

MID TONE
Neutral, atmospheric, mixture of low and high
Acoustic guitar or tenor saxophone
Bay, cardamom, coriander, fennel, rosemary, thyme

HIGH TONE
Bright, acidic, sunny, high, refreshing
Piccolo or triangle
Cilantro, basil, citrus zest, dill, lemongrass, lime leaf, tarragon, marjoram, parsley, shiso

When you are working with aromatics, it's helpful to think about what you want to add to the dish and which tonal direction you want to take with it. The reason why cilantro and lime work so well with avocado is that there are rich, vegetal notes in addition to mild earthy and bittersweet notes. The high tones of cilantro and lime brighten and lift the flavor. Imagine putting fresh oregano in guacamole. Wrong, right? The tone of oregano is too low, too woodsy and floral—it just doesn't work to balance the avocado.

This is not to say that high-toned herbs such as basil cannot be combined successfully with bright, acidic ingredients like tomatoes, but think about the greater context of the dish and also lean heavily on culinary tradition for guidance. Oregano, a low-toned herb, works with tomato by balancing it. Basil is bright and high-toned, lifting a sauce higher, but when combined with beef in a Bolognese and the triple hit of grounding umami, it all works. There are no hard rules with this stuff, but if you know what space an ingredient occupies, you are better able to figure out whether it's appropriate to include. Think about a dinner party you want to throw: You don't invite all attention-seeking narcissists—hopefully just one at most. If you invite a few, there have to be enough selfless souls that are excellent listeners to balance the mood and save your dinner.

> **FUN FACT** Saffron, unlike the majority of herbs and spices that are primarily soluble in oil, is water-soluble. "Bloom" saffron in a little water or stock to bring out the color and flavor before adding it to a dish.

Cooking with Herbs

How to cook with herbs depends on if you are using fresh or dried. Let's first tackle fresh. Have you ever seen a bartender smack a fresh mint leaf before adding it to a cocktail? This is to release the aromatics so that the oils can more quickly and easily be infused into a drink. You can do the same with fresh herbs in your cooking. Check out the Sweet Potato Soup on page 105, and you'll see I advise smacking the lime leaves around before adding them to the soup. In quick-cooking dishes, this is an easy way to maximize the impact of herbs, especially ones like lime leaves, fresh bay, or curry leaves that are sturdier in texture and therefore stingier about releasing essential oils.

For longer-cooked dishes, you can use fresh herbs both at the start of cooking and as a refresher at the end. Many cuisines rely on herbs and spices to be layered to allow for the flavor to slowly develop over time. Cilantro, for example, added early to simmering beans, will mellow with time, tasting lightly bright and vegetal while losing some of its bolder characteristics. But a refresher of the herb either as a garnish or stirred in at the end, shows off its fresher, bolder side. I use this technique often, especially with parsley and cilantro stems, which are as delicious as their leaf counterpart but need a little time to soften and cook down (see page 118).

Most home cooks use an insignificant amount of fresh herbs in their dishes. Unless you're following one of the recipes in this book or those by a chef who specializes in bold herb and spice flavors in their cooking, consider doubling or tripling the amount of fresh, tender herbs called for in most recipes. Very rarely will this increase result in any kind of imbalance. What's much more likely is that it will result in a fresher, brighter, more delicious dish. I will kick any recipe out of my life that calls for a measly 1 tablespoon of fresh parsley. You should too. Of course, generally speaking, woodier herbs like rosemary, savory, oregano, lavender, and marjoram can overwhelm a dish because of their very strong flavor profile, so you don't want to go over-board with those. Also, tarragon is great, but a little goes a long way. However, always be more liberal with your use of fresh basil, cilantro, parsley, thyme, chervil, dill, and mint; it's very hard to use too much.

Dried herbs must be handled differently. It's best to add dried herbs early in the cooking process to allow them to rehydrate and to soften their harsher, more concentrated qualities. If using dried herbs (I give suggestions on page 116 as to which ones are worthwhile), they are best for longer-cooking dishes. A sprinkling of dried herbs in a soup right before serving does little to improve its complexity and will likely result in textural problems (crunchy, papery bits of . . . what is that? hay?).

What if you're one of those people who calls cilantro the "devil's weed" and you think it tastes like soap? When is the right time to add soap to your cooking? Science has recently discovered that this reaction is not just a personal quirk, giving cilantro haters data to back up their distaste. Geneticists for 23andMe, using a sample size of 25,000, cross-referenced the cilantro haters with their genetics and found a spot near odor-detecting genes (including one with proximity to a gene known to recognize the soapiness in cilantro's aroma) that suggests cilantro distaste may come from variants in olfactory receptors.[25] Despite the genetic connection, the researchers reported that studies showed hatred for cilantro has only a minor underlying genetic component, and people can still learn to love, or at least tolerate, the stuff.

SUBSTITUTING FRESH HERBS FOR DRIED

RATIO	3 parts fresh herb to 1 part dried
EXAMPLE	1 tablespoon fresh thyme leaves to 1 teaspoon dried thyme

The Skinny on Dried Herbs

I'll be frank with you: I'm not a big fan of dried herbs because most of them are poor substitutes for their fresh counterparts, losing much of their oomph and flavor through drying and storing. I do, however, have exceptions to this hard-line stance and recognize that the convenience factor of dried herbs is high. Herbs that grow in hot, dry climates have aromatics that can withstand low-water conditions; this includes thyme, rosemary, oregano, and bay laurel. Such aromatics are held in the dried matter of the leaves far better than more temperate herbs. Simply compare the flavor of dried rosemary to dried parsley to see for yourself which one retains its flavor better. So feel free to use oregano, marjoram, bay, thyme, rosemary, sage, or savory in either dried or fresh forms.

Now, pull up a chair and let's have a heart-to-heart about dried parsley, basil, and cilantro. I'm not going to waste a second here: these three herbs in dried form are bullshit ingredients and not worth your money. If you don't want to buy a fresh bunch every time you need a little, I highly recommend a small container garden of these three herbs so they are always on hand.

Herbs are dried many ways: in the sun, in a dehydrator, in a low-heat oven, in a microwave, in a cool, dark place, and freeze-dried. Some of these, like freeze-drying and microwaving, work better than others because less of the good stuff is lost in the process. "The basic dilemma," says Harold McGee in his excellent book *On Food and Cooking*, "is that many aroma chemicals are more volatile than water, so any process that evaporates most of the water will also evaporate most of the flavor." Markets are starting to sell freeze-dried herbs, and I would recommend them over other dried options.

Chopping Fresh Herbs

I'll never forget when my mentor, James Beard award–winning chef Jerry Traunfeld, scolded us line cooks for overmincing our herbs. He'd stand over our shoulders, see the dark green mash of chopped herbs on our boards, collect himself and then through gritted teeth explain how the mashing of the herbs into a black sludge destroys the flavor, releasing the aromatics into the air and onto the cutting board. He'd go on to explain how the flavor needed to be released when the diner bit into the herb or as it melded into the dish—the knife and cutting board weren't paying top dollar to appreciate ten courses at the Herbfarm Restaurant, known for its creative use of all the fresh herbs grown on the property.

When I'm making a dish with multiple fresh herbs, I like to leave them bigger so that the flavor combinations are more complex. With your first bite you might get mint and basil, your second bite basil and cilantro, and your third bite all three. To see exactly how to prep and chop herbs, check out this video I made: bit.ly/2qAp2bB. I made another demonstrating the best way to store herbs: bit.ly/2pa3npq.

PARSLEY	Use parsley stems when making vegetable stock; store them in a ziplock bag in the freezer along with vegetable scraps.
CILANTRO	Use cilantro stems in Latin or Vietnamese stocks, or chop them fine to use in guacamole or tacos. Use them in marinades, like in the Fiery Roasted Thai Chile Chicken Wings on page 167.
BOTH	Use both in Italian Salsa Verde (page 45) or in a chimichurri recipe. Puree or chop the stems with oil and freeze in ice cube trays; use to finish off soups.

Freezing Herbs

If you don't know who J. Kenji López-Alt is, you need to. He's the author of *The Food Lab* and the managing culinary director at Serious Eats, my go-to online source for practical food science. López-Alt tested out various ways of freezing herbs and found that freezing chopped fresh herbs in oil—either in ice cube trays or packed flat in ziplock bags—preserved herb flavor the best.[26] Remember, though, these herbs will still not equal the flavor and texture of fresh. His tests were done on herbs that had been frozen for two weeks.

When I've personally frozen leftover pesto and salsa verde, I top them off with oil and pack into (labeled!) plastic pint containers; if used within six months there is only a small loss of flavor. Another way to freeze pesto and other herb sauces is on a parchment-lined baking sheet. Just spread the sauce out, freeze it on the tray, and then break it into the desired portions (for thicker spreads you can score it prior to freezing to make portioning easier). Slip each one into a freezer bag and seal it tightly, getting as much air out as possible.

A few other tips for using up leftover herbs:

1 Leftover thyme or parsley can be tucked into freezer bags for making stock. When you notice that thyme in your crisper drawer and you have no immediate plans to use it, go ahead and throw it in the freezer. Next time you are cooking, add carrot peels and tops, onion cores, and celery ends to the bag. Make your compost work for you.

2 Throw mint and parsley into smoothies for a boost of brightness.

3 Throw them in everywhere, actually, but especially on salads, grain dishes, or roasted vegetables.

PACKAGED HERB PASTES

I've tried those tubes of processed herbs before just to see what was what, and I can tell you that they are inferior to what you can easily produce in your own kitchen and freeze for later. Many of them contain sugar and preservatives, plus they are pricey to boot. If you're going on a long sea voyage or if you live in a place with few options for buying fresh herbs, it's better than no herbs at all (or dusty dried herbs from the Pleistocene Epoch), but for anyone with three minutes to spare to chop some basil, I give this tubular form of herb delivery system a thumbs down.

Spices

If herbs are potent, spices can be lethal; I'm not talking about chiles here, but the whole range of seeds, bark, berries, and roots that are used to add interest to food. Spices have medicinal and healing properties and—if used with an inexperienced hand—can tip a dish toward bitterness. It bears repeating what I said earlier: you can make food taste good without using spices if you focus on the proper deployment of salt, acid, sweet, fat, bitter, and umami. Spices can lift dishes to greatness but are more typically the cause of imbalance in a dish. As an illustration, I'll never forget when my wonderful, generous wife cooked me dinner one night (as mentioned, she is not a regular cook) and reached for turmeric and lavender to finish a pot of rice. An amateur painter, she later told me that the colors drew her in. The lurid splashes of color spiraled through the dish dared me to take a bite. I said, "You first," when she told me what she had added. "Uh, HELL NO," she replied, "it's all for you."

I don't mean to scare you off from spices; there is no greater joy for the cook than to walk through a spice market or shop, be taken in by the aroma of a dozen cuisines, and get carried away by the palette of possibilities. So let's learn the basics, so that you can confidently reach for saffron, smoked paprika, lavender, and turmeric, but maybe not all at once. And if you have not yet done the Spiced Carrot Salad experiment on page 29, I highly recommend you do before venturing forth into the world of spices.

I'm sure you've heard that whole spices are better than preground spices, and I'm here to tell you the exact same thing, because it's true. Volatile aromas in spices are released when they are crushed or ground. Light and oxygen exposure further degrade the flavor. Keeping spices whole preserves the essential oils until you are ready to release them, so purchasing them this way is ideal. All the same, I recognize that the convenience factor of ground spices is high. If you do buy them preground, be sure to store them correctly for maximum potency (see page 123) and buy them from reputable sources with a high turnover of inventory.

Did you know that you can grind cardamom pods without breaking them open and separating the little black seeds from the husk? Simply pop the whole pods into a spice grinder and grind it up fine. If you're following a recipe, use just a wee bit more to compensate for the slightly less flavorful ground husk. Would you now like to know how to get back the hours of your life you spent opening pods and separating seed from husk? Me too.

Toasting Spices

Toasting spices, typically in a dry pan, does a few important things:

- Due to chemical reactions that produce new compounds, toasting changes the flavor of a spice, making it more complex. This simultaneously shaves off the spice's harsher edges, mellowing it in the process. For example, the slight bitter notes of raw cumin seed are softened, and its earthy qualities are mellowed and deepened.

- It evaporates off any excess moisture and makes the spices crisper, allowing for easier grinding.

- It kills any potential unwanted bacterial "friends." This is especially important when using a spice blend without further cooking. Many spices for purchase have already been treated for this via irradiation, pasteurization, or with the gas ethylene oxide, but not all are, and it's hard to know what may have been contaminated.[27]

If you're making a spice mixture, like the Sri Lankan one for the lamb recipe on page 133, be sure to let the spices cool completely before crushing them in a spice grinder or mortar and pestle, lest the grinding release the fragile aromatics prematurely.

You need not toast spices in all cases. If you are crusting a steak with a spice blend, there is no need for toasting, as searing or grilling the meat will take care of that step. Just remember: at some point in the life of spices in your kitchen, a tour of a hot pan and/or comingling with hot fat are the way to go. There is no need to dry-toast already ground spices, as the increased surface area will evaporate off volatile aromas and you are likely to burn them in the process. As López-Alt says, "If you smell it while you're cooking it, it will *not* be in your food when you serve it." Add them to the cooking fat along with onions or other ingredients to both offer protection and a medium to absorb the flavor.

When to Add Spices

There is no perfect time to add spices to a dish because it really depends on what spice and whether it is ground, whole, toasted, or not. Very generally speaking, lean on adding most spices early in the process to allow them time to develop and deepen with cooking. That being said, if you toast your spices and grind them or cook them whole in a little oil, a sprinkling of them at the end of cooking can be lovely. Examples of this include toasted coriander and cumin sprinkled over huevos rancheros; toasted fennel and coriander sprinkled over roasted squash or carrots; oil-roasted cumin and mustard seeds mixed into roasted potatoes; and garam masala stirred into a curry at the beginning and end.

Certain spices are perfectly fine being sprinkled on food right from the jar, no toasting required. Sumac—a lemony tart, mildly earthy spice from the berry of the non-poisonous sumac bush—would be a prime example. I sprinkle it liberally over a romaine, feta, and toasted pita salad known as fattoush, and over baba ghanoush and hummus.

WHERE TO BUY SPICES

- A dedicated spice shop. In Seattle, we are lucky enough to have World Spice. Maybe you have someplace similar near you.
- Online from a reputable spice dealer, such as World Spice, Penzeys, the Spice Trader, or Kalustyan's.
- Your local supermarket or ethnic grocery that has a spice section with high turnover, ideally sold in bulk bins.

WHERE NEVER TO BUY SPICES

- In a jar at a bargain supermarket on some closeout sale. Why not? Because they may or may not have gotten them from an estate sale. I kid, but they are most likely very old. Some deals are just not worth it: no one ever bragged about the good deal they got on spices or condoms.

BEST STORAGE SPOT

- In the freezer in a well-sealed glass container, where they can stay "fresh" for a few years, but you may need to evaporate off any trapped condensation by toasting them a bit.

SECOND-BEST (AND MORE REALISTIC) STORAGE SPOT

- In opaque, well-sealed jars in a cool, dark place. Buy in super small quantities so you are constantly replenishing with the freshest spices possible.

Herb and Spice Substitutions

Remember when I said you need to know what space an ingredient occupies so that you can better know how to add it to a dish? Well, knowing your ingredients also helps you be a champ when it comes to substitutions. So instead of asking what you can use to substitute for lime leaf, ask yourself what space does lime leaf occupy, using the lessons you've learned in this book. Here, I'll help you with this one. Lime leaf is an aromatic herb that can be used to infuse a floral, lime flavor to food. It is not bitter. It is not acidic. So lime juice would get us some of the lime flavor but would add acidity that might create an imbalance in your dish. Lime zest, if the pith is carefully avoided, is not bitter and contains lovely aromatic oils. Bingo.

Let's try a few more: A recipe calls for shiso leaf, one of my favorite herbs. Also known as Japanese mint, shiso is truly unique but when you get to know it, you realize that it has flavors reminiscent of mint and Thai basil, with a whiff of cilantro and just a little bit of heat. Not a perfect replacement, but a bit of a few of those would get you closer.

Your grandmother's tomato sauce recipe calls for fennel seeds and you're standing in the spice section of your local market and the dad with the stroller rolls over your foot to take the last tablespoon from the bulk container. You're able to grab a lonely fennel seed off the counter and taste it to decide what a good substitute would be. It's licorice-y for sure. So is star anise and anise seed . . . hmmm, would one of those work? But fennel seed is also a little bit sweet. You could add a star anise pod and just a touch of honey to both bump up the sweetness and counteract the slight bitterness that star anise sometimes has.

Last one: A recipe calls for smoked paprika and you don't have it. What do you think you could use as a substitute? Think about it for a second before reading on. Smoked paprika is a bittersweet, fairly mild ground chile with a distinctive smoky flavor. I would substitute regular paprika plus a little bit of smoked salt (take away a little salt in the recipe) or ancho chile powder (mild and lightly smoky). Don't have either of those? Try a little regular paprika plus a tiny pinch of chipotle chile powder (much spicier and smoky). You get the idea, right?

OK, but what if you simply don't know what the ingredient tastes like? In some ways, that's a good problem to have because it means there is something new and fun to learn. A quick Google search should reveal the basic flavor profile of the herb or spice and help you narrow down a good replacement.

BEGUILING BAY

My friend Ian wasn't sure what the hell bay leaf was actually doing to his food all these years, so I suggested he grind one leaf with a tablespoon of sugar in a spice grinder and taste it to know what it has been contributing. When I talk about bay leaf I'm talking specifically about bay laurel (*Laurus nobilis*) and not what is often sold in stores as California bay (*Umbellularia*). Bay laurel is a lovely, lightly spicy-sweet, slightly floral, menthol-like, highly undervalued herb. I use it in desserts and savory dishes. California bay is a completely different animal: the leaves are longer, duller, and pointier, and it has an unpleasant kerosene-like aroma and flavor. You will often find bay laurel in dried form and the icky California bay in the fresh form.

My response to Ian's curiosity can be applied to any herb or spice. If you're unsure how an aromatic is contributing to your food and you don't want to chew it up on its own, combine it with sugar (or salt, if you prefer) in a spice grinder, grind it up, and taste it. Now you will know what that ingredient is adding flavorwise to a dish. (Keep in mind, however, that the flavor will mellow as it cooks.) See for yourself! Some suggestions to try: star anise, curry leaf, juniper, fenugreek, and cardamom.

Replacing Herbs and Spices

I'm sure you've heard that you should replace all your dried herbs and spices every six months. Maybe you've been told to do this annually. Either way, I'm not a fan of black-and-white rules (except that you should never buy dried parsley, cilantro, and basil—I'm dead serious about that). So, my advice is that it depends. Take a whiff. Does it smell like dust? Hay? Nothing? Pitch it. Does it still have a pungent and fresh aroma? Keep it. But here's a better suggestion for you. Next time a recipe calls for an herb or spice you don't normally cook with, take the exact measurement of what you need and write it on your shopping list. Grab your measuring spoons and head to a market near you that has a bulk section. Measure exactly what you need for the recipe into the little bags or a container you bring with you. When you go to cook, all you need to do is dump the amount in. Both efficient and easy, you will be using the freshest spices and herbs possible. For aromatics you use more often, buy extra, but if possible, buy in bulk, in smaller quantities, at a place that has frequent turnover.

Extracting the Most Flavor from Aromatics

Even though herbal teas are very popular, water is not the best substance (technically known as a "solvent") to bring out the character of spices and herbs. Fat is the best, but having an herbal lard tea doesn't appeal. Alcohol is second best (especially strong alcohols), making all those citrus-infused vodkas and basil- or fennel-infused gin cocktails more than just menu marketing schtick.

Practically speaking, when cooking, you want to expose the aromatics to fat. This shouldn't be too hard, as most recipes start with a little bit of fat. Deglazing with alcohol also helps to release any alcohol-soluble molecules in the aromatics.

Spice Grinder

Pros: Easy, convenient, consistent texture

Cons: The grinder can break, heat generated from using the machine may heat up the spices if ground too long (releasing volatile aromas), cleanup requires some effort (I recommend cleaning by running kosher salt through the grinder)

Recommended brand: Krups F203 3-ounce Electric Spice and Coffee Grinder

Mortar and Pestle

Pros: Makes you feel like a stud for grinding spices with just the power of your big guns, less heat applied to the spices, easy cleanup

Cons: Hard work, inconsistent texture

Recommended brand: Vasconia 4-cup Granite Molcajete

How to Fix an Over-Aromatized Dish

Let's say you like sage but you got a little heavy-handed with it when you were making a pan sauce. What are you going to do now that it's ten minutes until dinner? This is where I'd ask you exactly what the worst effect of the sage is for you. If it's bitterness, then you already know a bit more salt or a touch of sweetness will help tone that down. If it's truly the total package flavor of sage, then you have a few options (listed here in the order you should attempt them):

1   Dull the flavor by adding fat to coat the tongue. Swirl in more butter or hit it with a little cream.
2   Add bulk or dilute by adding more of everything else.
3   Distract by adding another complementary herb—say thyme here—to throw attention over to a different set of flavor notes.

Scaling Up Herbs and Spices

So you want to make a big batch of a dish that calls for herbs or spices or both. Do you scale these ingredients exactly the same way as you would the amount of chicken called for? I checked in with Raghavan Iyer, author of numerous Indian cuisine cookbooks, and he's of the opinion that herbs and spices should be scaled up identically: "to maintain the balance [of the original recipe] you have to keep the flavor proportions the same." But home cooks I reached out to had disaster stories of big-batch stews bullied by cumin, of rosemary gone wild, of cloves burning holes through their tongues.

Here's my take on the matter: when you are working with a tried-and-true recipe from a trusted source, scaling up herbs and spices exactly as written maintains the balance and keeps the recipe true to the flavor profile intended by the author. Especially with things like Indian curries, where the balance of spices is the backbone of the whole dish, if not the entire cuisine.

But what about something like a pot roast? The initial recipe calls for a spice rub containing rosemary and chiles. Say you enjoy rosemary but don't love it and you scale up the pot roast recipe four times. The surface area increase of the larger chunk of pot roast is not proportional to the increase in the spice rub. So when you rub that quadrupled rosemary-chile rub on the exterior, it's going on very, very thick. When you take a bite with the outer "crust" of that roast, you're going to get a much bigger hit of rosemary and heat. So you absolutely need to consider what kind of dish you are multiplying before making the call.

Raghavan, in his experience working with commercial recipes, advises that ingredients bringing heat, such as chiles and peppercorns, should only be scaled up 50 to 60 percent and salt scaled up about 75 percent. Heat and salt are much easier to add than dial back. My additional suggestion here is that if you are using an ingredient that you like in small doses but are not a huge fan of, ease off on it when scaling up recipes. Personally, I back away from numbing ingredients like cloves when batching recipes. I can always add more later, and it's worthwhile to not risk overdoing it, even if the flavor will be slightly different with less time for that spice to mellow.

An even better suggestion? Don't scale up any recipe that you haven't first tried and enjoyed.

Smoke

I'm a big fan of using smoke as an ingredient. Ideally the smoke comes from real wood in a smoker or grill, but that's not an everyday or even every month option for many home cooks. I use smoke a couple of different ways when I can't get outside. Smoked salt is a fantastic ingredient and I use it often to impart the aromatic of the outdoors into my food. Smoked paprika and chipotle powder are in regular rotation as well. Cooking with bacon is an indirect form of using smoke as an aromatic. For vegetarians, a pinch of finely ground lapsang souchong tea is your new best friend. I sauté onions with the tea to impart a bacon-like flavor to a dish.

Smoke doesn't always have to be wood smoke to produce fantastic aromas. I'm a little embarrassed by this now because it reeks of insecure showmanship, but way back when, I came up with a sweet pea soup that used dry ice to convey the scent of mint up to the diner's nose. I also had a version developed with my friend chef Dana Cree that used a strong cinnamon tea for a roasted parsnip soup with apple butter.

Citrus Zest

Watch a bartender strip an orange twist into a drink; they always do it over the drink itself and never onto a cutting board—or at least, the good ones don't. When you zest citrus, volatile aromatics are released in the form of oils. If you do this over your cutting board, the wood will taste and smell fantastic. For best flavor, zest directly over a dish and eyeball the amount using the following as a guide: 1 medium lemon will yield about 1 tablespoon zest. Need 1 teaspoon of zest? Zest one-third of that lemon. Limes yield 1 scant tablespoon. An average orange yields roughly 2 tablespoons zest. To preserve the delicate aromatics and a bright freshness, add citrus zest to a dish in the later part of cooking.

Combining Aromatics

Most importantly, if you are new to cooking or unsure about flavor combinations, lean heavily on the combined wisdom of the cuisines of the world, as innumerable cooks throughout history have figured out what goes best with what and when. There are whole books on this topic alone, and rather than give you insufficient information, I will refer you to the best resources out there for ingredient and flavor combinations. *The Flavor Bible* by Karen Page and Andrew Dornenburg is a great resource. Also check out FoodPairing.com, a website that uses science to suggest ingredient combinations.

Aromatics and Leftovers

Is it true that leftovers taste better the next day? It depends. Simple dishes without aromatics (mac and cheese) will probably taste the same, but a braised meat dish with layers of herbs and spices will indeed taste better. The first day you make it, it certainly tastes good, but astute tasters will notice that each flavor is a bit distinct and separate from the next. Aromatic ingredients undergo a multitude of reactions as they mix and mingle with the ingredients they are cooked with—as the dish cools and sits and then gets reheated, the aromatics mellow. The next day, the dish has changed for the better, growing more cohesive, complex, and rounded. You know what else makes it better the next day? All you had to do was reheat it.

Experiment Time

Lesson: Learn to identify tonal categories of herbs and spices. Aromatics to use (make sure they are fresh):
- Cardamom pods (have a friend crush it up a bit)
- Fresh mint, lightly smacked between your palms
- Ground cinnamon
- Cumin seeds
- Coriander seeds, lightly crushed
- Smoked paprika
- Fresh cilantro, lightly smacked between your palms
- Fresh or dried orange peel

Method: Get a friend to blindfold you. Be sure you can trust them. Have them put a spice or herb right under your nose. First, try to guess what it is you are smelling. Don't be discouraged if you fail miserably. It's much harder than you would think, even knowing the possible choices at the outset. Then, whether you know what the herb or spice is or not, tell your friend to put each one into one of three categorical spots. On the left is low tone (earthy, smoky, funky), in the center is mid tone (neutral, a little low, a little high), and on the right is high tone (bright, light, citrusy, sunny).

Conclusion: Even if you had no idea what you were smelling, I bet you will get most of the tones correct.

Becky says: *Low tone (cinnamon, cumin, smoked paprika), mid tone (cardamom, coriander), high tone (mint, cilantro, orange peel).*

Experiment Time

Lesson: How the flavor profile of spices changes after toasting.

Materials needed: 1 teaspoon fennel seeds, 1 teaspoon coriander seeds.

Method: Smell and taste a fennel seed and write down your thoughts on aroma and flavor. Then, in a dry sauté pan, add 1 teaspoon fennel seeds and cook over medium heat until they are fragrant and lightly toasted. Dump them onto a plate and smell them immediately. Note your thoughts on aroma. Now try a few. How has the flavor changed?

Becky says: *Raw fennel has a light licorice scent and the flavor is bittersweet with notes of licorice. Toasted fennel smells of butterscotch and light licorice. The flavor is less bitter and more sweet than raw fennel, while still tasting of licorice.*

Now do this same experiment with coriander seeds. What is the aroma and flavor pre-toasting versus post?

Becky says: *Raw coriander aroma is very faintly citrus and the flavor is of earth, cilantro, floral, and lavender. Toasted coriander aroma smells of popcorn and citrus. Toasted coriander flavor tastes nutty, lightly floral, slightly citrusy, and like peanut brittle and popcorn.*

Sri Lankan Spiced Rack of Lamb with Coconut Milk Sauce

MAKES 4 SERVINGS

An aromatic spice crust surrounds beautiful medium-rare lamb chops that float on a pool of creamy, savory coconut milk sauce. Garnish the chops with crispy fried curry leaves, also known as your new favorite herb. Serve this with rice and, optionally, some Pickled Mangoes (page 135) on the side. So many aspects of aromatics are in this dish: from the spice rub to the aromatized coconut milk to the nutty, spicy fried herb garnish. If you do serve this dish with the mangoes, you will get a crash course in the diversity and excitement of cooking with aromatics.

- 2 dried chiles de árbol
- 1 cinnamon stick
- ¼ cup coriander seeds
- 2 tablespoons cumin seeds
- 1 tablespoon fine sea salt, plus more for seasoning
- 1 teaspoon uncooked white rice
- 1 teaspoon brown mustard seeds
- 1 teaspoon fennel seeds
- 1 teaspoon green cardamom pods
- ½ teaspoon fenugreek seeds
- 3 whole cloves

- 1½ cups fresh (or frozen) curry leaves (found at Asian markets), divided
- 1 frenched rack of lamb
- 2 tablespoons high-heat oil, such as avocado, divided
- 1 (13½-ounce) can unsweetened coconut milk
- 1 tablespoon freshly squeezed lemon juice
- 1 teaspoon fish sauce

1 Preheat the oven to 350 degrees F.

2 While wearing gloves, break up the chiles and cinnamon into smaller pieces. Add to a spice grinder along with the coriander, cumin, sea salt, rice, mustard seeds, fennel seeds, cardamom, fenugreek, cloves, and ½ cup of the curry leaves. Finely grind the mixture and coat the lamb with the rub. You may need to do this in two batches.

3 Heat 1 tablespoon of the oil in an ovenproof skillet (preferably cast-iron) over medium-high heat. Sear the lamb rack, turning several times, until the spices have browned, being

careful not to burn them. Transfer the skillet to the oven and roast the rack until it reaches an internal temperature of 125 to 135 degrees F for rare to medium-rare. Once the lamb reaches the desired temperature, transfer it from the pan to a clean tray or platter and cover loosely with foil, allowing it to rest for 15 minutes.

4 Meanwhile, heat the remaining 1 tablespoon oil in the same skillet over medium-high heat. Add the remaining 1 cup curry leaves and stir them in the oil until crisp. Transfer them to a paper towel to drain and sprinkle with a little sea salt. Add the coconut milk to the pan (do not wipe first), along with any juices from the lamb resting tray. Simmer the coconut milk until it reduces in volume by one-third, about 7 minutes. Add the lemon juice and fish sauce. Taste the sauce and add more salt or lemon juice if needed. To serve, pool some sauce in a bowl. Cut the lamb rack into chops and serve them on top of the coconut milk sauce. Garnish with fried curry leaves on top of the lamb.

Pickled Mangoes MAKES 6 SERVINGS

I made a version of this quick pickle for my friend Tanmeet Sethi. It was inspired by Indian cuisine and similar pickles I'd had before. I was a little nervous to see her reaction. She enjoyed it but cautiously noted, "If you want it to be more authentically Indian, double the spices." "All of them?" I gasped, my whiteness never more glaring. I did and I've never looked back—it was so much better. More than two times better. Serve these mangoes with the Sri Lankan lamb recipe (page 133) or try them on fish tacos.

- 2 cups peeled semi-ripe mango, cut into strips
- 1 tablespoon kosher salt
- 3 tablespoons coconut oil
- 2 tablespoons fennel seeds, lightly ground
- 2 tablespoons cumin seeds, lightly ground
- 2 teaspoons brown mustard seeds
- 2 teaspoons turmeric powder
- 2 teaspoons red pepper flakes

1 In a colander, mix the mango with the salt and let sit for 30 minutes. Lightly rinse the mango and leave in the colander to drain.

2 Meanwhile, in a large skillet, heat the coconut oil for 20 seconds or so over medium heat. Add all the spices and stir until the seeds pop and the spices are fragrant, about 1 minute. Toss the spiced oil with the mango. Serve immediately or refrigerate and use within 1 week.

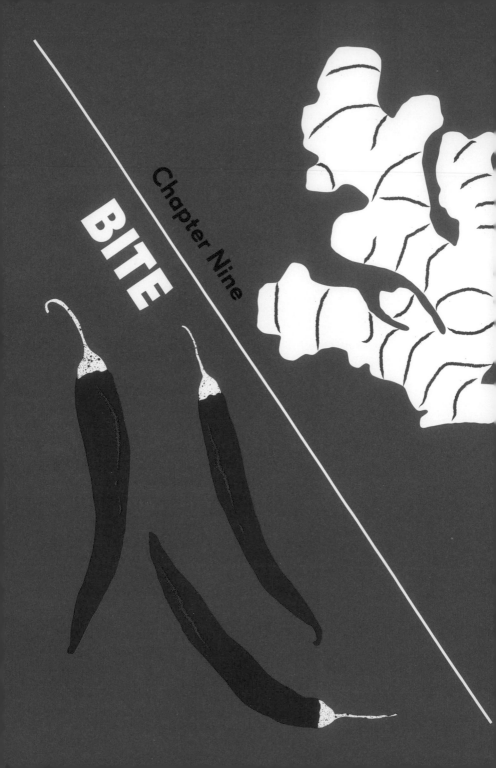

Chapter Nine

BITE

You might not think you're a masochist, but if you love the feeling of your mouth and nasal passages being assaulted by chiles, garlic, horseradish, and similar ingredients, you're actually the textbook definition of the word (minus the kink). Masochism can be defined as having a "taste for suffering," and if you've ever been that person sweating and drooling your way through ten-alarm wings or Sichuan cuisine, then you have a thing for pain. The suffering you experience while eating hot chiles, for example, is not a taste per se, it's more like the sensation of getting sucker punched in the face.

This sensation of heat, or rather pungency, has its roots in two different groups of chemicals. One group, thiocyanates—found in mustard plants and relatives (including wasabi and horseradish)—are light and small and quickly escape from these bitey ingredients when grated or cut. This is why wasabi and horseradish go straight to your nose, causing pain and mischief when they get there. The other group of chemicals, alkylamides, are found in chiles, ginger, peppercorns, and Sichuan pepper. Instead of quickly heading for your nasal passages, these heavier chemicals sit on your tongue and torture you there.

What exactly is happening when you're sweating and crying while you eat something exceptionally hot? As soon as your trigeminal nerve, the A-train between your tongue and nasal cavity and your brain, recognizes what you've done, it goes on high alert. Now comes the pain, and in the case of chile heat, an attempt to cool your body down (sweating). Some of the compounds that fire the trigeminal nerve are capsaicin (chile peppers), gingerol (ginger root), piperine (black pepper), and allyl isothiocyanate (horseradish). The trigeminal nerve is also responsible for sensing temperature and touch. Other parts of your body respond similarly to the assault on your tongue: your nasal cavity, under your fingernails, the surface of your eye. This reaction is called *chemesthesis*, which is a fancy word meaning "HOLY CRAP, FIRE IN THE HOLE!" Command central to body: "*Release everything!* Fire tears, sweat, snot, and drool!"

Dr. Barry Green of the John B. Pierce Laboratory explained in *Scientific American* that capsaicin also "stimulates the nerves that respond only to mild increases in temperature—the ones that give the sensation of moderate warmth. So capsaicin sends two messages to the brain: 'I am an intense stimulus,' and 'I am warmth.'" This explains why the chile you just ate might be ice cold out of the fridge but you register it as physical heat in your mouth. The trigeminal nerve and chemesthesis are also responsible for both numbness and the "cooling" effect of menthol (which stimulates nerves that register cold temperatures). Sichuan peppercorn—not an actual peppercorn at all, but related to citrus—tingles your lips and tongue, and if used in large quantities, it numbs your palate. Cloves provide a similar numbing sensation, which is why clove oil has been used to treat dental pain since medieval times.

The effects we get from eating ingredients with "bite" are often trippy (like feeling that chiles are heat hot when they're not), mildly uncomfortable (like tongue numbness—just try a flower known as a "buzz button"), or truly painful (chile oil in the eye anyone?). So why do we keep going back to the well for more? What's in it for us? In short, it makes our food exciting. Thrill-seekers especially love playing with these extreme food reactions. But there's also some science behind our pleasure in discomfort. Two words: endorphins and dopamine, aka the brain's happy juice. Endorphins block the nerve's ability to keep sending pain signals; dopamine fills us with pleasurable feelings. Also, some people simply feel the pain much more acutely than others. Tolerant tasters are more likely to be chile-heads just as you'd be hard pressed to find many sensitive tasters eating hot peppers for sport. You can train yourself to tolerate chiles, similar to how exposure to bitterness can alter your tolerance to certain ingredients. Culture and peer pressure, plus adding a little sugar to your chile as is done in Mexico to spicy lollipops (these are great!), can move you toward greater acceptance of ingredients with bite.

The trick to cooking with ingredients with bite, whether it is chiles or numbing cloves, is to allow them to flavor the dish and tingle or excite your palate without overwhelming you or causing actual pain—unless that's your thing and no judgment here. Using another music analogy: if a song is being played way too loud, you may become overwhelmed, overstimulated, and unable to pull out a lyric or any subtlety in tone. The experience is therefore limited, perhaps painfully so. This same thing happens with food. Once again, it's all about balance. When you're able to give someone a fun ride with bitey ingredients *and* they can still appreciate the entire dish, you have earned your stripes.

Chiles

From the full-throated burning assault of the hottest chiles to the light, fruity hit of the most mild, cooks and eaters around the world reach for chiles when they want something to heat up and grab their palate. Black peppercorns used to fill this role but chiles have relegated them to a more old-school form of bite. Chiles are now king.

Scoville Scale and Chile Heat Classification

We can thank Wilbur Scoville, or "Hot Pants" as I like to call him, for the scale developed in 1912 to give us a basic idea of how hot we can expect a pepper to be. To be fair, it's not a completely accurate tool, as it's based on testers' individual sensitivity to capsaicin, which is variable. Other scales are more accurate, namely high-performance liquid chromatography, which is a highfalutin way of measuring how many parts per million of the exact alkaloids that cause chile heat exist in the tested pepper.

For a cook's purposes, it's best to think of chile peppers in the following categories:

1 Sweet (bell, pimento)
2 Mild (shishito, anaheim, poblano, paprika)
3 Medium-mild (jalapeño, padron)
4 Medium (jalapeño, New Mexico/Hatch, guajillo/mirasol)
5 Medium-hot (jalapeño, serrano)
6 Hot (arbol, cayenne, Thai bird)
7 Holy crap hot (habanero, scotch bonnet)
8 Hotter than *%#&@ are you insane? (ghost pepper, Trinidad Moruga Scorpion, Carolina Reaper)
9 Pepper spray
10 Pure capsaicin
11 DEATH

CHILE FLAVOR CATEGORIES

If a recipe calls for one of these chiles and you need to make a substitute, stay within the flavor category and check the heat level of the chile you want to use (you may need to use a smaller amount of a spicier pepper). I've listed some of my favorite chiles from left to right in order of their heat.

- Fruity: Guajillo, aji amarillo, Thai, habanero
- Smoky: Ancho (smoked poblano), chipotle (smoked jalapeño)
- Vegetal/Grassy: Poblano, anaheim, patron, shishito, jalapeño, serrano

You may have noticed that jalapeños are in three of my made-up heat categories—what gives? Jalapeños can, as one seed catalog advertised, have a Scoville rating from 1,000 to between 15,000 and 20,000 depending on the cultivar. Astute readers might anticipate what ingredient category I would put jalapeños in generally, and you'd be right: they are *absolutely* a bullshit ingredient. Which is a pity because I really like jalapeños. But what I love more than jalapeños is the *idea* of jalapeños—the notion of a chile pepper with a grassy, bright flavor profile and heat that is noticeable yet fairly mild. That jalapeño does not exist in our world in any kind of predictable way anymore. "Young man, you over there, the supermarket produce worker—pray tell, which cultivar of jalapeño is this so I know how spicy it's going to be?" You see the problem. Some have pointed to the popularity of commercially produced frozen mild jalapeño poppers that have infiltrated a market where spicier cultivars used to reign supreme, but I've been unable to back up this chile gossip with a trusted source. Either way, the jalapeño's reputation has certainly been tarnished. Esteemed food writer Nancy Leson calls them *haole* (white people) peppers in her house because of how mild they can be, and journalist Marc Ramirez dubbed them *haolepeños*. When a recipe calls for jalapeño I do a 1:1 substitution with serranos, which are smaller and very consistent in heat.

FUN FACT The Carolina Reaper chile pepper, which is one of the hottest in the world and measures in at about 1.5 million Scoville units, is grown by the PuckerButt Pepper Company.

Working with Fresh and Dried Chiles

Fresh chiles are easy to work with: simply clean them, chop them up (wear gloves!), and cook with them or add to salsas or salads. You get extra flavor credit for charring them whole over a flame, under a broiler, on a grill, or in a skillet. Charring adds a complex, toasty note to the base flavor.

Dried chiles have incredible flavor and are super convenient, and for these reasons they are my more typical go-to when I reach for heat. The drying process concentrates the flavor compounds, giving the chiles aromas reminiscent of dried fruits. If smoke is used in the drying process, there is yet another layer of aromatics.

To get the best flavor out of dried chiles, first toast them in one of the following ways:

1   For a few chiles: Place them in a dry pan over medium-high heat and cook, turning frequently, for 3 to 4 minutes, or until puffed, pliable, and fragrant.

2   For large batches: Preheat the oven to 350 degrees F, spread the chiles on a baking sheet, and bake, turning occasionally, for about 10 minutes, or until puffed, pliable, and fragrant.

3   In a microwave: Spread the chiles on a plate and nuke on high in 15-second intervals for about 30 seconds total, or until pliable and fragrant.

Cleaning Chiles

I find it easier to clean dried chiles after toasting them because they've puffed up a bit, making it easier to snip the stem off. Shake out the seeds and for less heat, pull out the membranes, if possible (wear gloves!). Dried chiles, once cleaned, are ready to rehydrate; simply add to hot water for 10 to 15 minutes. Use both the chiles and the rehydration liquid in chile pastes, sauces, moles, and hot sauce. The chiles can also be added in pieces to braises or soups or be ground into a chile powder. Charred fresh chiles can be chopped and used as is or demembraned and deseeded for less heat.

To watch a video demonstrating the toasting, cleaning, and grinding process for dried chiles, visit bit.ly/2pGrHAs.

SUBSTITUTION RATIOS FOR WHOLE AND GROUND CHILES

If a recipe calls for a rehydrated whole dried chile and you only have a fresh one, you can substitute one for one, though you will be losing a little of the deeper, more complex flavor that comes from the drying process, especially if it's a smoked chile (in that case you'll want to char the fresh chile for sure). Caveat: This is not a perfect science because the heat of chiles varies from chile to chile (see the jalapeño discussion on page 140). Taste as you go when using hot chiles—add some, taste, then add some more.

- For each dried or fresh large whole chile, substitute 1 heaping tablespoon dried chile powder. *Example: 1 dried ancho chile: 1 heaping tablespoon ancho chile powder*
- For each dried or fresh medium whole chile, substitute 2 teaspoons dried chile powder. *Example: 1 dried chipotle chile: 2 teaspoons chipotle chile powder*
- For each dried or fresh small whole chile, substitute ½ teaspoon dried chile powder. *Example: 1 dried cayenne pepper: ½ teaspoon cayenne powder*

All of the Flavor, Less of the Pain

It's much easier to add more heat than retract it. If you know you are cooking for a mixed crowd (chile warriors, chile wimps, and everyone in between), simply provide red pepper flakes or chopped fresh chiles in small bowls at the table. If you want to make a soup, curry, or chili and imbue the whole dish with the flavor and heat of hotter chiles, separate out a mild batch early on and cook it in a small pot for heat-averse friends.

If you want chile flavor in your dish but less of the pain, here are some tips:

1   Remove the membranes (the ribs, or whitish bits that anchor the seeds). The membranes are the hottest part

of a chile, so keep that in mind for trivia night at your local bar or when your uncle tells you the heat is all in the seeds. He's not completely wrong, as capsaicin can get onto the seeds and inner walls of the pepper, but that happens as a result of proximity and not because the heat was there from the get-go. For greatest heat reduction, remove the capsaicin-contaminated seeds as well. By the way, the membranes can contribute bitter notes to a dish, so removing them also tamps this down.

2   Add red pepper flakes or chile powder at the end of cooking to add a burst of heat versus allowing the capsaicin to permeate the entire dish by tossing them in at the start.

3   Put chiles in a soup, sauce, or stew whole—without cutting them open—to keep the membrane from mingling with the liquid. Sometimes I'll put fresh chiles I've cut a slit into in a cheesecloth bag; as I cook and taste, I have a bit more control and can pull the bag out when I've achieved the heat level and flavor desired. See an example of this technique in the Sweet Potato Soup on page 105.

If you trip and end up tipping too much cayenne into your soup, stew, or stir-fry—and now it's *en fuego* and you happen to have dinner guests arriving in twenty minutes—breathe and try not to panic. Here are some possible solutions, in order of priority:

1   Dairy, specifically the casein in mammal's milk (soy and nut milks aren't as effective), binds with capsaicin, lifting it off the tongue and toning it down while bringing relief to the palate. Stir in cream, if it makes sense for the dish, or add more cheese. Top with sour cream or yogurt, or if all else fails, pour milk at the table. There is a reason ice-cold raita (yogurt with cooling mint and cucumber) is served with hot Indian curries.

2   Capsaicin is fat-soluble, so adding olive oil or another source of fat to the dish can help a bit. This is especially

good to remember if you don't want to add dairy. Some swear by the addition of nut butters (where it makes sense) to a dish to ease the heat.

3   Distract the palate from the fire of a thousand suns by sweetening the deal. Honey, sugar, fruit juice, whatever you've got. You'll find habanero, a very hot but fruity pepper, balanced in hot sauces with mango or other fruits. If you're concerned the dish will get too sweet, you can add vinegar or citrus to rebalance it. The all-purpose dipping sauce in Vietnamese cuisine called *nuoc cham* (see a recipe on page 165) is a perfectly balanced mixture of hot chiles, lime juice, sugar, and fish sauce. Though hot, the sweet, salt, and acid act as balancers, toning down the perception of the sauce's heat. Vietnamese and Thai cuisines are quintessential studies in this kind of balance.

4   Add bulk to the dish by adding more of the other ingredients, spreading the heat over a greater volume.

5   Serve the hot dish with a starch such as plain bread or rice to compensate for the heat.

What doesn't work very well is panicking and guzzling water. Capsaicin is not water-soluble, so drinking water does an efficient job of spreading the pain around your mouth. Maybe your friend suggests beer because she heard alcohol can dissolve capsaicin. While true, and an ice-cold beer with your five-star Thai red curry chicken sounds marvelous, there's simply not enough alcohol in beer or even in a cocktail to dissolve capsaicin. If someone's offering bathtub moonshine, though, say yes.

911 for Chile Burns

You gotta love *Cook's Illustrated*. They actually got volunteers to rub chiles on their skin and in their mouths so they could test out various remedies to ease the pain. Here's what they found:

> It turns out that peroxide reacts with capsaicin molecules, changing their structure and rendering them incapable of bonding with our receptors. Peroxide works even better in the presence of a base like baking soda: We found that a solution of ⅛ teaspoon of baking soda, 1 tablespoon of water, and 1 tablespoon of hydrogen peroxide could be used to wash the affected area or as a mouthwash (swish vigorously for 30 seconds) to tone down a chile's stinging burn to a mild warmth.

If you're somewhere with no hydrogen peroxide and baking soda, a method that I've personally test-driven and can vouch for (when I touched my lips after chopping Thai chiles while cooking for a client) involves these steps: First, wash the affected area with soap and a little water (the soap breaks up the capsaicin oil). Next, dab the area with either rubbing alcohol or, in a pinch, use tequila, gin, or vodka (it's all I had!). Finally, rub yogurt or sour cream on the area; it will feel soothing, or at least it soothed me when my client walked in the door and found me sitting in a chair, sweating, with yogurt all over my lips.

Karyn Schwartz, owner of the herb and spice apothecary Sugar Pill in Seattle, advised me on how to get chile burn out of your eyes in case you find yourself, as I did, having rubbed them after chopping serranos without wearing gloves. (Did I mention how important it is to wear gloves when chopping hot chiles?) The fix she told me about is just as crazy as it sounds: it's called "sweeping," and you use your own long hair—or grab anyone's near you—and sweep it through your eye. The natural oils on hair strands will adhere to some of the capsaicin molecules. Rub more hair over your eyelids until the intensity subsides. She learned this firsthand after a gallon jar of cayenne opened onto her face when she reached up onto a high shelf for it. Or, if you have short hair like me (or no hair), throw a shot of milk into your eyes. Trust me, your dignity is already long gone.

While we are talking about cautionary chile tales, make sure that you first fry fresh chiles in a little oil to mitigate some of the heat before putting them into a blender. If you don't, you could clear out a whole neighborhood block when making a particularly hot chile paste or sauce.

Scaling Up Recipes with Chiles

My advice is to avoid a straight scaling up of chiles for the simple reason that many types of chiles are inconsistent in their heat level (I'm looking at you, jalapeños). You don't want to find out after adding twenty-eight chiles into a big-batch chili recipe that you rolled the dice and got the hottest jalapeños of the bunch. If a recipe calls for three serranos and you're tripling the recipe, start with maybe four or five and then taste as you go. You can always add more.

Culinary instructor and author Karen Jurgensen told me that she scales up mild chiles proportionately but holds back on the hot ones. She also goes easy on cloves and ground white pepper, because "it seems that cloves can take over—the flavor doesn't dissipate as quickly." Like chiles, too much of any ingredient with bite can wreck your palate.

BUSTING CHILE MYTHS

Can you tell how hot a chile is going to be without tasting it?

No, you can't really tell exactly how hot a chile is going to be by smelling it, noting how pointy it is, counting ridges or scar lines, holding it to your ear and hoping it will speak to you, or any other thing you may have heard or imagined. But you can cut the stem off and lightly touch it to your tongue. It's almost like taking a bite but with way less pain.

Can eating chiles "ruin" your taste buds?

No. We've already learned that hot chiles don't affect your taste buds but rather nerves related to temperature and pain detection. Paul Bosland, director of the Chile Pepper Institute at New Mexico State University, says that the numbness that occurs even after eating a Trinidad Moruga Scorpion pepper, one of the spiciest peppers on record, usually dissipates within twenty-four hours.[28]

CHILLI, CHILI, OR CHILE?

The spelling of the word *chile* is all over the place, and much of it depends on where in the world you live. Here is your quick and dirty guide to what's what in the United States when it comes to this word:

- Chilli: Only OK if you're in the UK.
- Chili: As in chili con carne, the mild-to-spicy meat, tomato, and bean stew, but whoops, not always with beans because according to some, that's blasphemous.
- Chili's: An American casual dining restaurant chain that features Tex-Mex-style cuisine.
- Chile: A country in South America, and also the flavorful peppers that add fruitiness, smokiness, vegetal, or earthy flavors to our food, in addition to varying levels of heat.

And while we are being pedantic, adorable cooking teacher and author Raghavan Iyer takes umbrage with using the word "spicy" to refer to heat at all. He implores us to "keep the word 'spicy' to aromatic spices."

Garlic and Onions

It wouldn't be far off to say that if cuisine were a house, garlic and onions would be the foundation. Or at least, that's how most cuisines revere the "stinking rose," which is not really a rose, but a name for members of the pungent and diverse allium family. I can hear you wondering, "We are all the way into Chapter 9 and you're just *now* pouring the foundation of our cuisine house?"

Alliums are indeed wondrous additions to cuisine, able to provide sweetness, sharpness, and savoriness, all dependent on how they are cooked, chopped, or preserved. I put them in the Bite chapter because, outside of really well-cooked garlic and onions, this family has an instantly recognizable sharp, palate-grabbing bite. But are they in fact the foundation of great food? I would place them in a similar camp to aromatics (and they are, in fact, quite aromatic). In short, I believe many cooks approach their food with a sort of checklist, prioritizing big, bold flavors: Garlic! Chiles! Spices! They check them off while perhaps neglecting much more important keys to a great dish, which are the ingredient quality, proper salt deployment, acidity level, sweetness, fat, bitterness, and umami. I've eaten dishes so bludgeoned with raw garlic they left a chemical trail. I've seen more salads than I can count bullied by far too many slices of raw onion, the more delicate ingredients obliterated. Like chiles, garlic and onion have a very important place, but cooks need to be careful and respect the power that these ingredients have.

Biological Warfare

When a bug, bird, or mammal such as yourself bites into a clove of garlic, it's the opening salvo of a biochemical engagement. The cells of the garlic become damaged by your teeth (or the knife) and two molecules join together: the amino acid alliin and the enzyme alliinase. They make sweet, sweet love and produce allicin. Allicin causes vampires to quake in their capes.

The garlic variety, growing conditions, and type of fat it is cooked in (butter is mellowing whereas unsaturated vegetable oils bring out more assertive garlic flavors) are important to how powerful it is, especially garlic that isn't cooked for very long. Just as important is how you cut, mash, or slice a garlic clove. The more abuse the garlic clove takes, the stronger allicin becomes—and the more potent, bitey, and intense the garlic.

> **FUN FACT** Only chumps brush their teeth in an attempt to get rid of persistent garlic breath—turns out it doesn't help much at all. Professional garlic breathers reach for raw apples, lettuce, or mint leaves. All are high in phenolic compounds, which are the aromatic compounds that react with the ones in garlic that are causing your fiery death breath. All three are also high in the enzymes polyphenol oxidase and reductase, which are believed to speed up reactions, escorting the garlic vapor away faster.[29]

Daniel Gritzer put garlic through a number of mincing and mashing tests to determine how potency was affected. What he found was that grating garlic was the fastest way to create a noxiously pungent, juicy raw garlic, as it most effectively breaks down the cells, creating allicin in spades. Mincing seemed to be the best overall technique (and I agree) since the cells were broken down minimally as compared to a grater or garlic press, allowing for little sharp bites of raw garlic while generally containing the fury of the garlic gods. When cooked, knife-minced garlic didn't burn as quickly as grated or pressed; it also became sweet and more mellow.[30]

The Changing Flavor of Raw Garlic

Listed in order of potency, from most to least, what follows is how the flavor, texture, and best application of raw garlic changes depending on how it's chopped (or not):

- **Grated:** burns easily, noxious, juicy, best for aiolis
- **Pressed:** mildly juicy, less noxious than grated, not as efficient (you lose some to the device), burns easily
- **Hand-chopped:** potent, versatile, less likely to burn, sweeter when cooked
- **Sliced:** great for infusing sauces or braising
- **Whole, crushed:** great for infusing into oils or sauces, mild

But what if you want to use garlic raw or very lightly cooked and you don't want all that pungency and bite? You can rinse it! Mince or slice the garlic, put it in a sieve, and rinse it with lukewarm water. A lot of the allicin goes down the drain and the garlic instantly has less bite.

The Changing Flavor of Cooked Garlic

Listed in order of potency, from most to least, what follows is how the flavor of garlic changes depending on how it's cooked:

- **Cooked too fast, dark-brown to burnt:** bitter notes, acrid (discard it)
- **Slowly and gently cooked in vegetable oil:** potent, hot, sweetens a bit
- **Slowly and gently cooked in butter:** harsh edges soften, heat softens, sweetens a bit
- **Browned until soft:** caramel notes, sweeter, mild, no heat
- **Roasted until very soft:** very sweet, toasty, mellow, buttery, mild

To maximize the garlic flavor in garlic-centric dishes, use it in multiple ways to create a layering effect. Infuse crushed whole cloves in oil or butter by heating the fat slowly until the garlic sizzles, cooking it gently for 10 minutes, straining out the garlic (discard it), and then using that oil to cook your food. You can add more minced garlic with the main ingredients and cook it for a while. In the last 20 minutes of cooking, gild the lily by stirring in some paper-thin garlic slices. You'll get the sweet mellowness of the well-integrated garlic, plus a gentle bite from the quick-cooked slices, without being overwhelmed by a complete and utter garlic takedown.

Do be mindful of how you cut and cook garlic, because it will affect the total balance of the dish. If you don't want too much bite, rinse it or cook it longer to mellow it; if you want a sharp bite, use it raw or cook only briefly. Unless you're making Fifty Clove of Garlic Soup, less is more.

Types of Garlic and Flavor Profiles

- **Hardneck:** If you've seen this type of garlic, it was most likely at a farmers' market in a cold climate where hardneck thrives. They are easily identified by their hard, woody central stalk. Bold, super bitey, and more aggressive than the softneck variety, garlic nuts go crazy for this variety and collect cultivars like baseball cards.

- **Softneck:** This is the type you are most likely to see in just about every grocery store; it has many more cloves than hardneck varieties and a bit less bite.

- **Elephant garlic (aka Buffalo garlic):** This milder garlic is not really a type of garlic at all, in fact, but a leek variant. Expect some oniony overtones and a large size (bigger than a baby's fist, smaller than an electric car). It's easy to peel and great slow-roasted until it's sticky-sweet.

- **Ramps:** The darling of chefs, ramps are wild foraged onions but I place them here for their garlic-like flavor. It's sweet and pungent and closely related to wild garlic. Ramps are fantastic in pasta dishes, grilled and eaten alongside steak, pickled, or thrown on a pizza with spring morels.

- **Green garlic:** Found mainly at farmers' markets, green garlic are immature garlic bulbs with the green tender tops attached, typically harvested in early spring. Cook them as you would leeks or scallions.

- **Garlic scapes:** Later in the spring, the green garlic top begins to twist and curl over several times prior to flowering. Farmers typically cut this off so more energy goes into the bulb but ingeniously started selling them to be used as a green vegetable. Infuse them into sauces, bake into bread puddings, or sauté for a pasta dish. They are a bit more sturdy than the tender green garlic.

- **Fermented black garlic:** If you've seen a shrink-wrapped package of garlic that looks like it came from the larder of the Wicked Witch of the West, then you've stumbled upon the "newest" form of garlic in the marketplace. Fermented black garlic is not actually fermented (can't we name anything accurately?); it's made by slowly drying and caramelizing the bulb over several weeks. The result is a sweet, fudgy, rich, but mild garlic flavor that lingers. It has notes of truffle, mushroom, soy, and caramel. It's garlic that no longer has much bite left and perhaps would be better aligned with umami or sweet or maybe bitter. You see the issue here. Just give it a try; use it in sauces, vinaigrettes, or mixed with butter and melted over steak.

Types of Onions and Flavor Profiles

When I was in culinary school, I remember one of my chef-instructors asking me to grab him an onion, and when I got to the pantry, I was confronted with all the colors of the onion rainbow. I learned later, after I brought him one of everything, that if someone doesn't specify, they probably mean a yellow onion. What follows are a handful of the most common onions you may encounter.

- **Yellow/brown:** The cheapest onion, great for all manner of cooking, has quite a bite when raw, very sweet when caramelized
- **White:** Pungent, high water content, crisp, good in salsas
- **Red:** Pretty—especially when pickled, more mild than white or yellow, good on burgers and sandwiches or in salads
- **Sweet (Walla Walla, Vidalia, Maui):** Great raw, sweet, makes top-notch onion rings
- **Scallion/green onion:** Mild flavor; cooks quickly; less bite than yellow, white, or red; white parts contain the most intense flavor; green parts have a milder heat
- **Spring:** Immature bulb onion, more intense than scallions/green onions, white parts are better cooked, green parts can be minced and used raw
- **Cipollini:** Means "little onion" in Italian; thin-skinned; more sugar than yellow, white, or red; best roasted or caramelized
- **Shallot:** Chefs' favorite; mild, sweet, and crisp; less bite than yellow, white, or red; great in vinaigrettes and salads
- **Leek:** Mild, great in soups and stocks, mellow, buttery when braised, the sexy, luscious lady of the onion world
- **Pearl:** Bullshit onion; fresh ones require having infant thumbs to peel; frozen peeled ones are OK, I guess, but are not especially sweet or interesting, just very small; if you insist on using them, throw them in a martini or pair them with my other favorite annoying ingredients and make a bullshit salad out of spaghetti squash (watery), enoki mushrooms (pretty but tasteless), dandelion greens (so bitter!), and jalapeño (inconsistent heat)

Crybaby

When you cut an onion and break the cell walls, a series of chemical reactions causes a volatile sulfur compound (propanethial S-oxide) to be carried to the water in your eyes where the two mix to form, oh, nothing too bad, just *sulfuric acid*, which burns (because *acid*), which makes you cry to help wash it away. Go ahead and add garlic and onions to the list, along with stinging nettles, of "things we eat that are trying to destroy us."

To reduce the pungency of onions and their ability to make you cry, especially those that you will serve raw or pickled: after mincing or slicing, rinse them off with hot water to rid them of the tear-causing compounds (called *lacrimators*). Also, don't let onions sit for too long after cutting them; they get more pungent as they sit.

As for all the myths related to stopping your tears—everything from holding a match in your mouth to chewing gum to lighting a candle in the room (none of them work)—stick with science. The best possible anti-tear prevention, besides rinsing (which won't really help you while you are mid-chop), are goggles or contact lenses. Second best would be either using ice-cold onions, which slows down the chemical reactions, or running a fan to help redirect the fumes. Good cutting technique helps as well because if you cut the onion, realize the chunks are too big, and then go Benihana on it, you're going to crush a lot of cell walls. So measure twice, cut once, or in cooking terms: practice those knife skills! I show you how to cut and slice an onion properly here: bit.ly/2qAseEe.

Experience, by the way, does not toughen you up. Every once in a while I will cut an especially pungent onion and have to splash my face with water and wipe my eyes because I'm blotchy and red and blubbery like I just watched a *Brokeback Mountain/ Titanic/Schindler's List* movie marathon. The only way to deactivate the onion's chemical warfare is to apply heat to it; cooking inactivates the enzyme, so feel free to waggle your eyes over the pan with abandon and jeer at the onions, rendered impotent by fire and the ingenuity of humankind.

How to Fix a Dish Overpowered by Garlic or Onion

Sometimes the "bite" gets out of hand and you need to course correct; the following suggestions are listed in the order you should try them.

1   If possible, keep cooking the onions and garlic as they will mellow with time. Cooking breaks the pungent compound allicin down into various polysulfides. Allicin is alcohol-soluble; the polysulfides are fat-soluble. So . . . see 2.

2   Hedge your bets and be sure to add both fat and alcohol to the dish (if it makes sense) to help the compounds transform into softer, kinder, less bitey versions of themselves.

3   For raw dishes that have been allium-bullied, take a note from the *nuoc cham* recipe on page 165, and add sugar or acid to distract from the spicy bite of the garlic or onion.

4   Add bulk or dilute by adding more of everything else, or make a separate, allium-free version of the recipe and mix the two together.

FUN FACT Many of the ingredients associated with "bite"—black peppercorns, chiles, and garlic—have antimicrobial properties. In one study, garlic killed 100 percent of the bacteria it encountered.[31]

My Culinary Nightmare

While alliums are revered the world over, I have something radical to tell you: you can still make great food without them. You might say I have some experience in this department. If I asked you what is the worst thing a chef could be allergic to, what would you say? That's right, garlic and onions. I developed a severe allergy to garlic (especially in raw form) and a milder allergy to onions fifteen years into my cooking career. It's like a joke, but it's not that funny. After I decided there was still a reason to live, I learned how to make my food so damn good without garlic or raw onions (I can tolerate them cooked) that my clients wouldn't even know it was missing. Impossible task? I thought so at first, but I used all the lessons in this book to create dishes that had all the elements in order—so much so that nothing would be missed. Now, of course I'm not talking about making garlicky chicken wings garlicky without garlic, but if the dish was not an overt garlic bomb, I would make sure the salt, acid, sweet, fat, bitter, umami, aromatics, other forms of bite, and texture were all dialed in. What was, on paper, a career-ending affliction turned into one of the inspirations for writing this book. Balance is more important than any one ingredient—even a family of ingredients, however beloved. I miss garlic. I miss raw shallots in a dressing. I miss onion rings. But I'm a better cook today than when I was rolling in garlic fries, puttanesca, kimchi, and (*sniff*) a great Caesar salad.

> I'm not saying there is a substitute for garlic that tastes just like garlic, but when I'm really missing it, I cook with a mixture I developed to approximate the many roles that garlic occupies in cuisine: the pronounced bite and pungency, the little bit of sweetness it gets when cooked, the intense aromatics that are heady like the best perfume, the earthy funk.

I use minced fennel (aromatic, similar texture, slight sweetness), a tiny bit of grated ginger (bite), a pinch of truffle salt (earthy, heady, funky), and a pinch of a spice called asafetida (the dried gum resin of an herb cultivated in India; sulfurous, funky). I sauté the mixture in a little oil until everything softens and mellows, and then I use it in place of garlic. You can employ a similar strategy if you are cooking for someone with an allergy. If you know all the things an ingredient is adding to the dish, you'll have a head start on finding a good substitute.

Ginger

Most of the ginger found in the marketplace is yellow ginger. At my local Japanese market I will sometimes see young (or new) ginger, which I buy when I want to make my own pickled ginger (gari).

The active components of ginger are gingerols and shogaols, both powerful and spicy when raw. Shogaols are much spicier than gingerols and are prevalent in dried ginger, which is why a little dried ginger goes a long way and is a somewhat different animal than fresh. If you must substitute fresh for dried or vice versa, use this ratio: 1 tablespoon freshly grated ginger to ¼ teaspoon ground ginger. When ginger is cooked, the compounds are converted into zingerone, a much milder compound that's slightly sweet. If the bite of ginger has gotten out of balance in a dish, add a bit more liquid and cook it longer to help mellow it out.

Other Ingredients with Bite

Wasabi, horseradish, radish, and mustard are four members of the Brassicaceae family. They're a brash, emotionally charged family, capable of really getting in your face. They'll bite your head off and leave you in tears but, as with all dysfunctional families, you can't help but keep going back for more.

The active, bitey compounds in wasabi, horseradish, and radish come alive when grated or cut. Mustard is activated when it's crushed or ground. These compounds are more water-soluble than those in chiles, meaning they hit you hard but leave you quickly, whereas chiles can torture you for a good long while. Wasabi heat and flavor are temporal, leaving the scene with urgency; they're at their most potent five to ten minutes after grating and then start to diminish soon after. This is why you'll often see wasabi in powdered form or in a paste.

Speaking of wasabi, you may already know this, but if you don't, I'm not going to spare your feelings. Most of the "wasabi" you think you are eating in sushi bars is not wasabi at all. It's green-colored horseradish with maybe a very small amount of real wasabi mixed in—but probably not. To be fair, horseradish and wasabi are similar, though wasabi is more subtle. Horseradish punches you in the nose; wasabi whispers sweet nothings in your ear first. Wasabi is much, much more expensive though, so most Americans are unfamiliar with it and would probably prefer what they've been eating and calling "wasabi" all along anyway.

FUN FACT The volatile compounds in wasabi are one reason sushi chefs put a little on the underside of the fish and on top of the rice. This sandwich effect protects the aroma (and the worst of the vaporous fumes) from escaping.

Daikon radish is a wonderful, often overlooked ingredient that's a bit less aggressive than some of the others we've discussed (chiles and raw garlic, specifically). I grate peeled daikon on a Microplane, squeeze out any liquid, and use the dried shavings as a refreshing zippy bite with fried tofu, atop grilled fish, or in soups. Alternatively, daikon can be cut into rounds and stewed or braised until it mellows and sweetens; it has a great sponge-like texture that absorbs whatever it's cooked in. If you've ever had a Vietnamese bánh mì sandwich, daikon was probably mixed with carrot, quick-pickled, and tucked into the roll to cut the fat of the pork. There are many types of radishes, but they all share a similar crisp, refreshing, slightly spicy bite. Whether you're eating French breakfast radishes with butter and salt, or thinly slicing the fantastically gorgeous watermelon radish into a salad, it's obvious to your palate when a radish grabs you by the tongue.

WASABI AND HORSERADISH 911

Here are a couple tips to reduce being nasally punched by wasabi or horseradish:

- Go easy, cowboy—if you blow out your nasal passages, you'll lose any subtlety in the rest of the dish. This is why sushi chefs wince internally when they see you mix wasabi into your soy sauce. They've already added the precise amount to the fish so that the wasabi complements the food but doesn't overwhelm it.
- Wasabi and horseradish can become painful when vapors hit the mucous membranes in your nasal passages. If you've taken in too much, breathe in through your nose and out through your mouth to clear out the active component that wants to rise off your tongue and go straight up your nose.

Mustard greens are truly underrated. Pickled, they are fantastic on a classic northern Thai curry called *khao soi*. Braised along with collard greens and kale, they add a bite and heat that make the greens far more interesting. Mustard seeds are used widely in German, French, and Scandinavian cuisine, and the pop and sizzle of mustard seeds in oil is inseparable from Indian cuisine. I love the bite of mustard "caviar" and always have a jar going in my fridge. It's super easy to make (see opposite page for a recipe) and great on top of braised meats, in salads, on cheese plates, or mixed into butter and smeared on a biscuit. There are literally endless ways to employ the bite and pop of mustard caviar.

MUSTARD CAVIAR

The preparation is super simple: Combine ½ cup yellow mustard seeds, ½ cup rice vinegar, ⅓ cup water, ⅓ cup mirin, 1 teaspoon granulated sugar, and ½ teaspoon sea salt in a small saucepan. Simmer gently for 45 minutes, or until the seeds plump up. Add more water if the liquid level gets low. Season to taste with fine sea salt. The caviar will keep in an airtight container in the fridge for a few weeks.

Storage Suggestions for Ingredients with Bite

- **Garlic and storage onions (yellow, white, red):** Keep in a paper bag with small holes punched out or in a basket in a cool, dark place with plenty of ventilation; don't store them with potatoes, since ethylene gas from the alliums will encourage the spuds to sprout.
- **Fresh onions, scallions, leeks, etc.:** Store these in your crisper drawer in a slightly open plastic bag and don't wash them until ready to use.
- **Ginger:** Keep it in a plastic bag in the crisper drawer, or in a well-sealed ziplock bag in the freezer so you can grate it frozen right when you need some.
- **(Real) wasabi:** Wrap each rhizome in a damp paper towel and place in an open plastic bag in the refrigerator. Re-wet the paper towel every few days as needed.
- **Radishes, including daikon:** Store in a slightly open bag in the crisper drawer and use within a week.
- **Mustard greens:** Keep them in a slightly open bag in the crisper drawer and don't wash until ready to use.

Peppercorns

We owe the flavor differences in various types of peppercorns to several factors: where they were grown, when the berries were picked (it's the fruit of a vine), and how they were processed.

Black

Black peppercorns are blanched and dried ripe green peppercorns that come from many different growing regions, all with slightly different flavor profiles. The two most well known are:

- Tellicherry, from Southern India, which is left on the vine to ripen longer than most black peppercorns. It is sweet-hot, with a deep, rich, well-rounded flavor.
- Lampong, a smaller peppercorn grown in Indonesia, is picked a bit earlier than Tellicherry. It is aromatic, citrusy, and sharp and has a hot punch that lingers.

If you were to only have one kind of black peppercorn, my recommendation would be for Tellicherry, as I find it to be more useful in a wide range of dishes. But truly, as long as you grind it fresh (the aromatics of all black peppercorns dissipate after about thirty minutes), any kind of black pepper will do. Save the expensive stuff for coating steaks or for Pasta alla Speranza (page 107), where you are better able to appreciate the aromatics and bite in quantity and without much competition from other ingredients.

Green

Green peppercorns are young, unripe "black" peppercorns. They are typically pickled, sometimes dried, and taste milder than black peppercorns while still packing a sharp punch. They are used in sauces and beloved in Thai cuisine.

White

Besides being the musty mothballs of the underworld to some, white peppercorns are black peppercorns that are fermented in water for up to two weeks to remove the fruit layer covering the seed. They are slightly less hot but far more funky, so people either love them or hate them. An informal survey of my colleagues revealed that many chefs don't care for white pepper, but not so for food writer and consultant Jacqueline Church, who blames the distaste on the fact that what most people have in their cupboard is super old. "We all know ground spices lose volatile compounds quickly. Fresh white pepper that was bottled this year—not last, not five years ago, not the year Betty White was born—is wonderful," she says.

Or perhaps she can't smell the chemical rotundone, found in spades in white pepper. Australian scientists studying the peppery notes of Shiraz stumbled upon this chemical and noted in their studies that 20 percent of people tested could not detect rotundone at all. When a wine has excess rotundone, it gives off aromas of "burned rubber," according to wine expert Jancis Robinson. White pepper has traditionally been used as a way to keep black peppercorn specks out of white foods in French cuisine, so its presence wasn't exactly motivated by flavor.

Pink and Sichuan

I love that these exist, mostly because there are two ways to know that the person you are talking to is pompously obsessed with food. Way #1: they tell you that a yam is really an orange sweet potato. Way #2: they make sure to tell you that pink and Sichuan peppercorns aren't actually peppercorns. I have done both many times, so I know. But did *you* know? Allow me to impress you.

Pink peppercorns come from a South American shrub. They are a little bit "peppery" (aha!) but I think of them more as a citrusy, floral, lightly sweet spice than as a means to add bite to foods. They are delicate, so use a grinder or mortar and pestle, as opposed to putting them in a peppermill.

Sichuan peppercorns are related to citrus. They tingle your lips and tongue and, if used in large quantities, numb your palate.

Jacqueline Church notes that Sichuan peppercorns "have the quality Chinese called 'má,' which translates as numbing—it has a tantalizing quality—and when combined with something spicy, or 'là,' it becomes 'málà': numbing and spicy. Chinese cuisine is brilliant at combining flavors—hot and sour, hot and sweet, numbing and spicy." A similar numbing spice to Sichuan peppercorn is a spice used in Japanese cuisine called *sansho*, where it's a component of *shichimi togarashi* (seven spice), among other uses. The active component is something called *sanshools*, and it thoroughly confuses your senses by simultaneously inducing touch sensitivity and a sense of something cool or cold. Eating Sichuan peppercorns or sansho and then contemplating the breezy electrical current running through your face is an underrated legal high. But, as with many bizarre and exciting things, a little goes a long way. Unless, of course, you're in Sichuan province, in which case hold on for the ride—it's electric!

A SALT AND PEPPER RANT

Dear every recipe, past and present:
I'm going to give it to you straight. "Season to taste with salt" needs to part ways with "and pepper." It's time for a divorce and it's going to be messy because the pair has been together for so long and people will balk at the inconvenience of having to see them at different times. Pepper is great but it never deserved equal billing simply by absorbing the reflected light of salt's brilliance. Salt is the key that unlocks the door, it's the light switch flipping on, it's the sun in the sky. Pepper is the optional scarf that looks good on some and really makes your eyes pop, but let's face it, sometimes it just clashes with that sweater—bad. Salt is almost never wrong and pepper is only sometimes right.

Experiment Time

The ever-present accompaniment to many Vietnamese dishes, *nuoc cham* is one of my most favorite sauces for its bold, bright, bitey brilliance. Much of what this book is about is contained in this sauce. Each element serves to balance the other: salty (fish sauce), sweet (sugar), sour (lime juice), umami (fish sauce), and bite (chiles and garlic). You'll have leftover sauce when this experiment is over. In lieu of making the homemade chile sauce for the Fiery Roasted Thai Chile Chicken Wings on page 167, use this as a dipping sauce or as a salad dressing (which is especially good over bowls of cold rice noodles with lots of fresh herbs, vegetables, and pork).

Lesson: Discover how sugar soothes the bite of chiles and how the way you chop garlic makes a difference in its potency.

Nuoc Cham MAKES 1 GENEROUS CUP

- ⅔ cup water
- ½ cup freshly squeezed lime juice (from about 3 limes)
- 2 tablespoons fish sauce
- 3 Thai chiles, minced, or 1 small serrano, minced (wear gloves!)
- 2 tablespoons finely shredded carrot (optional)
- 4 tablespoons granulated sugar, divided
- 2 small cloves garlic

1 In a measuring cup with a spout, whisk together the water, lime juice, fish sauce, minced chiles, and carrot. Divide the mixture equally into two small jars and label one #1 and the other #2. Into jar #1, add 2 tablespoons of the sugar and mix well until the sugar is dissolved.

2 Take a small taste of #1. Note how the chile and sugar are playing together. Now take a small taste of #2. Without the sugar, it should seem hotter and less balanced. When you feel like you have a good sense of what the sugar is doing for the

balance, go ahead and add the remaining 2 tablespoons sugar to jar #2 and mix well.

3 The next lesson is to show how the heat of garlic can change depending on how you cut it. Using a Microplane or other fine grater, grate exactly 1 teaspoon garlic and add it to jar #1. Using a knife, very finely mince and measure exactly 1 teaspoon garlic and add it to jar #2. Stir the contents of both jars well. Take a taste of each one and note how the garlic flavor is different. Cover both jars and place in the fridge. The next day, compare how the garlic flavor has changed in each sample. Combine them and use in recipes, after you've done your comparison evaluation. The sauce will keep in the fridge for 1 week.

Fiery Roasted Thai Chile Chicken Wings

MAKES 4 APPETIZER SERVINGS OR 2 MAIN DISH SERVINGS

This recipe features many bitey ingredients: garlic, ginger, black pepper, and chiles. For maximum flavor, coat the wings with the savory marinade paste a day in advance. Serve with Homemade Sweet Chile Sauce (or substitute Nuoc Cham, page 165) and plenty of jasmine rice or Thai sticky rice (and if you're wimpy, a tall glass of ice-cold milk).

- ½ cup chopped cilantro stems
- 4 cloves garlic
- 2 to 3 whole Thai chiles, or 1 teaspoon cayenne
- 3 tablespoons oyster sauce
- 2 tablespoons freshly grated ginger
- 1 tablespoon freshly ground black pepper
- 1 tablespoon fish sauce
- 2 teaspoons coriander seeds, toasted and ground
- 3 tablespoons high-heat oil, such as avocado, divided
- 2 pounds chicken wings (whole wings, if you can find them)
- Homemade Sweet Chile Sauce (recipe follows), for serving

1 Combine the cilantro, garlic, chiles, oyster sauce, ginger, black pepper, fish sauce, coriander, and 1 tablespoon of the oil in a food processor or blender until finely ground and well blended. Marinate the chicken with this paste for at least 1 hour but preferably overnight.
2 When you are ready to proceed with cooking, preheat the oven to 400 degrees F.
3 Line a baking sheet with parchment paper and brush it evenly with 1 tablespoon of the oil. Transfer the chicken wings, marinade and all, to the pan. Drizzle the remaining 1 tablespoon oil over the wings and roast until they are browned, crispy at the edges, and cooked through, 50 to 60 minutes. Serve with the chile sauce.

Homemade Sweet Chile Sauce MAKES ½ CUP

- ½ cup plus 2 tablespoons granulated sugar
- ½ cup rice vinegar
- ¼ cup water
- 3 tablespoons fish sauce
- 2 tablespoons sherry wine
- ½ to 1 tablespoon red pepper flakes (depending on desired heat)
- 3 cloves garlic, minced
- 1½ tablespoons cornstarch dissolved in ¼ cup cool water

1 Combine the sugar, vinegar, water, fish sauce, sherry, red pepper flakes, and garlic in a saucepan or pot. Bring to a rolling boil over high heat. Reduce the heat to medium and let boil for 10 minutes, or until reduced by half. Reduce the heat to low and add the cornstarch water mixture. Stir well to incorporate and continue stirring occasionally until the sauce thickens, about 2 minutes. Remove from the heat and taste. You should taste sweetness first, followed by sour, then spicy and salty notes. If the sauce isn't sweet enough, add a little more sugar. If it's not spicy enough, add more red pepper flakes. Cool completely and serve at room temperature or cold. It will last for several weeks in your refrigerator.

The Pantry's Southern-Style Hot Sauce MAKES 1 QUART

I teach classes at the Pantry, a cooking school in Seattle founded by my friend Brandi Henderson. This is the house hot sauce that we use in our recipes or offer at the table. In the summer when local farmers are flush with chiles, someone at the Pantry will be making a huge-ass batch of this hot sauce, flavorful with a range of peppers of varying heat levels. It's high on flavor, medium-mild in heat, and perfectly balanced with just enough acidity to brighten everything up. A jar of the hot sauce "accidentally" comes home with me a couple times a year. Don't tell Brandi.

- 1 pound red sweet chiles
- 13 ounces red medium chiles
- 3 ounces red hot chiles
- High-heat oil, such as avocado or rice bran

- 2 cups distilled white vinegar
- ¼ cup water
- 2 tablespoons granulated sugar
- 3½ teaspoons kosher salt

1 Preheat the oven broiler or a grill.
2 Trim the stems off the chiles and clean the chiles thoroughly. Toss them in enough oil to coat them. Roast them under the broiler or on the grill. The goal is to get a nice char on them, but not to cook them all the way; I like to see spots of black, but they should retain their bright color. Puree the roasted chiles (no need to peel) in a food processor or blender with enough of the vinegar to keep them moving.
3 Push the puree through a strainer, extracting as much of the pulp as possible. Add the water, sugar, salt, and the rest of the vinegar to the puree, cover, and chill in the fridge for a few days. (It can be used immediately, but it gets better with time.) After a few days, taste for adjustments. Refrigerated in an airtight container, the hot sauce will last for up to 1 year.

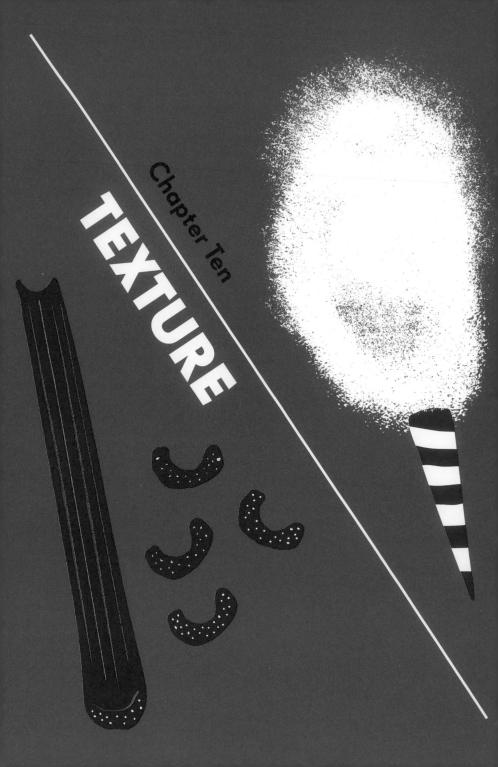

Chapter Ten

TEXTURE

'm going to give you a hypothetical. Let's say you've read this whole book, right up to this chapter. You've understood everything, you've done an experiment or two, you've thought about what it takes to get a dish right. You've got this. You invite your friends over and you make them a four-course meal where you are locked in on the salt, acid, sweet, bitter, fat, umami, aromatics, and bite. Everything is in perfect balance. You serve the entire meal, all four courses, as purees.

Question: does anyone come over to your house for dinner ever again? Allow me to answer that for you: no, unless they are a baby or compromised in the teeth department.

We crave texture in our food; more accurately, we crave a diversity of textures in our food. As omnivores we are drawn to using our teeth to grind, mash, and rip food like the animals we are. Texture is so important to our enjoyment of food that to break this rule is to ruin the dinner.

Think about how you feel when you see the word "crispy" or "creamy" on a menu. You imagine your teeth shattering through a piecrust or crunching through the exterior of fried chicken. And your tongue sensually coated with cold ice cream as it melts into a palate-pleasing liquid. Menu writers know this and gently guide (manipulate) you into selecting something that—without these evocative descriptors—you might not have ordered. Without the crunch and crisp of potato chips, and the sound it makes in your jaw that's carried into your eardrums, there would be little joy in these foods. Sure, the salt is great and the fat is pleasing, but we mostly crave the crunch.

FUN FACT Not only do humans like to chew, it's also good for us. A study found that older people who chew hard foods such as apples had a lower risk of losing their mental capabilities. Chewing increases blood flow to the brain, reducing the risk of dementia. "An apple a day" just took on a whole new level of importance.[32]

Texture 101

We have the trigeminal nerve to thank, once again, for our ability to detect the textures of foods. Anyone who owns a dog that sheds is already quite familiar with this nerve; its sensitivity is what causes you to pause while crunching through a handful of chips and reach into your mouth to remove a nearly invisible ¼-inch strand of dog hair. Even dogs themselves, who seem to be OK with eating dirt, rocks, and sand, can detect an unfamiliar texture. I once watched my black Labrador (RIP Bubba), famously known for her undiscriminating palate, work a tiny sprig of curly parsley I had given her for her death breath from the back of her mouth to the front and then onto the floor. I think the unusual texture was what made her spit it out, and the fact that it wasn't tempting as a food kept her from picking it back up. Everyone's a critic.

The texture of a food and how it interacts with our sensory nerves can affect our perception of the food's flavor. A puff of cotton candy might not seem nearly as sweet as the equivalent amount in granulated sugar. In cotton candy form, our perception of the sugar is somewhat locked up in fluffy, elusive sugar clouds, whereas in granulated sugar form it sits directly on our tongue with plenty of opportunity to interact with sweet receptors. This is why people who take capsaicin (or any number of bitter herbal medicines) medicinally do so in coated capsule form; the exterior of the capsule acts as a protective barrier, cutting out the sensory nerve middle man. Some things are best quickly ferried through our sensory receptors and nerves; it's the difference between a nonstop flight and an agonizingly painful three-city layover.

The more a food's texture approaches liquid form, the more intense the perception. A crab bisque might give you a bigger hit of crab flavor than the equivalent bite of crabmeat on its own because of the way the bisque lingers on your palate. When it comes to sauces, those with body are going to give you more sensory information than thin sauces, with some exceptions. A thin sauce generally passes over your tongue pretty quickly; it's gone before you know what happened. A sauce with body, like a demi-glace or beurre blanc, coats your tongue, spending serious quality time with your taste buds. Of course there is a downside to this extra time that a thicker sauce hangs around: if it's unbalanced or wildly over- or underseasoned you will be very aware of its faults. This is just one reason why in French cuisine, the *saucier* (sauce chef) is one of the most important cooks in the kitchen, if not *the* most important. One exception to the viscosity rule: the Vietnamese sauce *nuoc cham* (see the recipe on page 165) is very fluid, but because it's extremely intense and perfectly balanced, the bold flavor overpowers the speed at which it leaves your mouth.

Please don't go blending up all your food so that more of it fires your taste receptors. I only offer this information to show you the subtlety involved in matters of taste and texture. This is a terrible idea, but imagine blending up a bag of salt and vinegar potato chips: your perception would be that it's saltier, fattier, and even more acidic than its whole counterpart, even though it's not. Actually, this doesn't sound like such a terrible idea all of a sudden.

Gloopy, Gloppy, Slick, and Slimy

Foods that disgust or disturb you are most likely texture violations, especially in cultures that avoid a diversity of textures beyond creamy and crunchy. Think about the foods people are often turned off by: okra, cactus, mushrooms, eggplant, raw fish, the insides of tomatoes, egg yolks or underdone whites, tofu, natto, oysters. Many of these are mushy, mucousy, slimy, slippery, and/or spongy. Those not raised to appreciate such textures will be less likely to enjoy them.

> **FUN FACT** We eat with so much more than just our mouths. And I'm not talking about our eyes. If you rub your hand with sandpaper as you're eating something creamy like ice cream, you'll think the ice cream has a less creamy (if not gritty) texture. Conversely, you can enhance the texture of foods by touching something that evokes the desired texture. Try eating panna cotta while stroking cashmere or silk, or even eating ice cream while petting your cat (not a euphemism). Next, try not to sound like a freak as you explain what the hell you're doing when someone walks in on you.

Texture is culturally specific. In Japan and China many foods are part of the cuisine purely for their texture, over and above the flavor they may or may not provide. Fuchsia Dunlop, author of *Shark's Fin and Sichuan Pepper* (and many more excellent books), famously quipped that texture is the "last frontier for Westerners learning to appreciate Chinese food." Most non-Asian Westerners prefer creamy and crunchy things to gristly, bony, and gelatinous foods. And when food is slithery, bouncy, gloopy, or slimy, we really lose everyone else who wasn't born into a family that valued these textures. We tend to like the things we are familiar with.

In China they have a term for texture—*kou gan*—that is similar to our word *mouthfeel*. Kou gan is a highly celebrated aspect of Chinese cuisine and clearly evident if you've ever sampled sea cucumbers, goose intestines, chicken's feet, or pig's ears. It's all about the texture with these foods, and the enjoyment of them can be traced to both an appreciation of so-called nose-to-tail eating as well as the notion, often stemming from cuisines of the poor, that no bit should be wasted. But it can also be attributed to the tables of the wealthy where whole plates of goose feet were a luxury and delicacy that only the rich could amass in such quantity.

In Western cuisine, we have few dishes and ingredients we can point to that are similarly high in texture and low in flavor (though soul food of the American South such as okra, chitlins, and pig feet could be contenders). But the world over, it's not at all uncommon: in Japan there is natto, revered for its slimy, stringy texture, and tofu for its spongy silkiness. In the Philippines, there's balut—fertilized duck eggs that diners savor, crunching through little bones, while negotiating tiny feathers. In Thailand, night markets offer crunchy grasshoppers, cockroaches, and scorpions fried on sticks.

TEXTURAL CONTRAST

I think I knew instinctively at a young age that textural contrast makes boring food much more interesting. For much of my childhood, a peanut butter and jelly sandwich was daily fare. But one day when I was packing up my *Starsky and Hutch* lunchbox, instead of putting my little bag of potato chips on the side, I decided to open up my sandwich, scatter the chips inside, close the sandwich up, and eat it like that. Voila! The delightfully contrasting crunch in the middle of all that softness made for a much more interesting sandwich. Even as an adult, I sometimes still do this. (I write "sometimes" because I feel self-conscious, but "often" is the more honest word choice.)

Texture Is Contextual

Parmigiano-Reggiano has a graininess from amino acid crystals (*tyrosine*), a natural outcome of the aging process in well-made cheeses. These little crunchy crystals are desirable, but take that same texture and transplant it into a butter sauce and whoops, what happened? Ricotta is a fresh cheese that consists of curds that are separated out from the whey via an acidic ingredient such as buttermilk; the texture is great when you're expecting it. But take that same coagulated texture and imagine your cereal milk is curdled and yuck, you would reject it outright. Texture is also contextual based on in which decade you're serving the meal. My grandmother surely loved her asparagus aspic—wobbly, Technicolor jelly and all—but we were a few decades too young to appreciate it, despite being children of the Jell-O generation. Children are a bit phobic of new textures, but scientific studies show that expanding exposure to new textures at a young age helps future acceptance.[33] In other words, my grandmother was "helping" me when she made me choke down the evil jelly that oozed around the gefilte fish like *The Blob* (arguably a horror movie whose plot was one big, scary texture violation).

> **FUN FACT** Our palates are so sensitive that we can pick out ice crystals in ice cream measuring 40 microns (or $\frac{1}{25}$ millimeter). Ice cream made with liquid nitrogen freezes so fast that the crystal development is barely detectable, giving it an extraordinarily creamy texture.

Tannins and Texture

Have you ever sucked a tea bag? That sounds wrong. Let me start over: have you ever eaten an unripe Hachiya persimmon (the type that is acorn-shaped) and wondered what fresh puckery hell was happening to your tongue? I have, and I'll give you a report from the frontlines of that experience. In short: if I walked over to you, grabbed your tongue, and aggressively rubbed it down with a cheap terry-cloth towel, you'd have $\frac{1}{100}$ the experience. This is the power of tannins. Have I scared you away from ever trying Hachiya persimmons? I'm OK with that. But for you others, make sure it is mushy ripe before you eat it, or stick with Fuyu persimmons, which can be eaten at various stages of ripening, from crisp-hard to just barely soft, without sacrificing your tongue to the tannin gods.

Tannins are compounds (*polyphenols*) found in plant seeds, skins, stems, and bark. Tannins can be found in large quantities in trees (a main reason oak barrels are used to age wine), tea, grapes, walnut skins, dark chocolate, cinnamon (it's a bark, after all), cloves, and quince.

Tannins from oak were used to "tan" animal hides into leather. Imagine how powerful a substance must be to turn animal skin into leather. When you drink a Nebbiolo (a wine known for its intense tannins), it's a race to enjoy dinner before the tannins turn your mouth into a leather belt. Nebbiolos (Barolo) are some of the finest wines in the world—but they must be paired carefully with fatty, rich foods to be enjoyed without the terry-cloth towel sensation. Tannins can be aggressive but they also add complexity to food and wine. While there is an acidic component to tannins, the overarching effect is astringency or drying. This astringency can be a welcome aspect of wine, though, as it keeps the fruit from becoming cloying and helps cut the fat of rich foods.

I chatted about tannins with master sommelier Chris Tanghe and he stressed how the tannins in wine interact well with fat and protein, lifting the fat from the palate, enabling saliva to wash it away, and combining with proteins in such a way as to create a feeling of density and fullness. Tannins give wine a thickness and body they wouldn't have otherwise and also aid in preservation. As with all things, however, a little goes a long way. A smattering of walnuts (with their tannic skins) in a creamy, protein-rich salad resets the palate a bit and offers complexity and balance. A bowl of just walnuts? I don't know many people who enjoy snacking on them alone.

Near the end of my conversation with Chris, he said, "I'd be a terrible beaver," and I was like, "Huh? Come again?" He explained how beavers chew wood all day long and must be immune to the tannins. By contrast, he can't stand it when he's done with a lollipop or Popsicle and gets down to the stick because he hates the palate-drying astringency of the paper and wood. Now that's a discriminating palate—and exactly the guy you want choosing perfectly balanced wines for you.

Overcoming Texture Issues

Does your gag reflex get triggered when you eat certain foods? You'll want to skip to the next section because that's a serious texture aversion and my advice probably won't help, but for the rest of you who simply dislike the texture of mushrooms or think oysters are too slippery but you've only tried these foods a few times, keep reading.

First of all, let's debunk the myth that raw oysters need to be eaten whole, gulped down in a shooter, never meeting your teeth. That right there is a prescription for creating a food aversion, because what kind of evil food is so heinous it should not even be chewed? Chew your oysters! They are delicious and have more texture to them than if you just let them loll around on your tongue before swallowing. Mushroom haters who don't like the texture may have only eaten them when they were cooked improperly. I created a video on proper cooking technique for mushrooms that creates layers of texture and won't result in just a wet, squeaky, slimy, mess; watch it here: bit.ly/2qGiGXd.

Try slipping the texturally challenging ingredient into other foods so that you can slowly get used to the texture you dislike. Putting texture challenges into a burrito, dumpling, calzone, or similarly wrapped-up dish is a great way to introduce someone gradually to an ingredient that is intimidating otherwise. A breaded fried oyster is no problem for many who wouldn't go near a raw oyster. My wife doesn't like the texture of mushrooms or eggplant, so I've been slipping them into her food for ten years without telling her and she doesn't know! Until now. Shit.

Or try forming a new association in your mind with the texturally challenging food. If you like clams, but can't stomach raw oysters, think about chewing a clam while you eat the oyster. There is very little difference between a steamed clam and a raw oyster in texture. The clam is a bit chewier and the oyster is more wet and cold, but that's about it. This new association can really help you get over a texture aversion.

Using Texture to Add Interest

Next time you go out to dinner at a nice place, take note of the textural elements weaved into the dish. Rarely will you be served a beef stew with some mashed potatoes or a halibut curry over rice without a textural element for contrast. That stew might have crispy fried shallots sprinkled on top; the curry might have chopped scallions or chopped peanuts and chiles. When you start thinking like a chef, these "optional" garnishes don't seem so optional anymore but instead integral to providing the contrasts people crave. If you've ever had to endure a liquid diet, you will know from experience just how intense a craving for food texture can be. I bet when babies are crying inconsolably it's because they want a damn steak or some potato chips.

TEXTURE TYPES

CRISPY	Chips, roasted or fried pork or fish skin
CRUNCHY	Coriander seeds, vegetable chips, pretzels
POPPY	Caviar, mustard seeds, pomegranate seeds

continued on next page

CHEWY	Tripe, tendon, mushrooms, soft pretzels, tapioca pearls
SLIPPERY	Mushrooms, oysters, gelatin, seaweed
FLAKY	Pie crust, biscuits, croissants
SNAPPY	Sausages, fish cakes (*kamaboko*)
SPONGY	Tofu, sweetbreads, injera, pancakes
CREAMY	Ice cream, nut butters, milkshakes, soft cheeses
FLUFFY	Shaved ice, cotton candy
ASTRINGENT	Persimmon, quince, tannic wines, tea
TINGLY	Sichuan peppercorns, cloves, Pop Rocks, carbonated beverages

Experiment Time

Let's do a theoretical experiment to help you start thinking about texture differently. I'm going to give you a dish and you're going to come up with something you could *change* or *add* to the basic dish to make it more interesting texturally. After you've come up with what you'd do for each example, read my notes to see what I'd do.

Example: Pureed butternut squash soup
Answer: Here are some things I might garnish the soup with:
- Toasted pumpkin seeds
- Crostini chunks or serve whole crostini on the side
- Bits of amaretti (almond) cookie and toasted slivered almonds, as well as a drizzle of rosemary-infused cream
- Crispy pieces of prosciutto or country ham
- Thinly slivered crystalized ginger mixed with a small amount of fried sage

- Process the soup differently as only half pureed with half left chunky—especially if other dishes in the meal are creamy

Dish 1: Bibb lettuce salad with goat cheese and pears

Becky says: *I might garnish with maple-glazed crunchy walnuts or pomegranate seeds or croutons made from either a sweet raisin bread or a date-nut bread.*

Dish 2: Fish tacos (grilled fish in soft corn tortillas)

Becky says: *I might make a crispy slaw of jicama, unripe mango, and cilantro or a chunky salsa with bits of chiles, fresh tomatoes, herbs, and sweet onion. Or maybe change the preparation by battering and frying the fish instead, topping with a slaw or salsa, and then serving with a creamy guacamole for contrast. Another idea would be to pull the skin off the grilled fish, bake it until crisp, and sprinkle the crispy skin pieces on top of the fish to add crunch and variety (this is especially great with salmon). Check out my video for that technique here: bit.ly/2pZD5dt.*

Dish 3: Pan-seared shrimp and grits

Becky says: *Let's look to what another chef would do with this example: Richard Doering of Bristol Bar & Grille in Louisville, Kentucky, adds pieces of green apple to the shrimp sauté and chunks of country ham to a sorghum-bourbon demi-glace that accompanies the dish. With this transformation, you've gone from textures of toothsome shrimp (not chewy or bouncy, unless they are overcooked) and creamy grits to toothsome shrimp, creamy grits, velvety demi-glace, crisp apples, and chewy ham—far more textures, far more interest.*

Texturally Superior BLAT MAKES 1 SANDWICH

The BLT is one of the most perfectly engineered sandwiches and brings together a lot of the elements of taste and flavor we've covered. Adding an avocado to the BLT to turn it into the not-quite-as-nice-sounding BLAT is a pure stroke of creamy, textural genius.

Warning: *I have a lot of rules for making the BLAT right (see opposite page). They're important for success. Don't go any further with building your sandwich until you've read them all. Twice. Maybe even could recite them from memory.*

- 2 slices of sourdough or other white bread (no thicker than ½ inch)
- 2 tablespoons Best Foods or other quality mayonnaise (not Miracle Whip!)
- 2 leaves of very cold fresh iceberg lettuce
- ½ perfectly ripe avocado, cut into thin slices
- 2 slices of the best, ripest, most awesomely delicious tomato
- 2 slices of best-quality ¼-inch-thick bacon, perfectly cooked

1 Toast the bread, but only on one side. (I like having the toasted side face the fillings—it's the best of both worlds, a softer texture to sink your teeth into and caramelization and crunch inside.) Toast that one side under a broiler or in a skillet so it's uniformly brown and crispy. (I add a bit of olive oil to the pan and then place a small cast-iron skillet on top of the bread to keep it in even contact with the skillet.)

2 Spread the mayonnaise evenly over the toasted side of both bread slices and make sure you get it all the way to the edges. The fat in the mayo acts as a water-resistant raincoat, protecting the toast from getting soggy.

3 Lay a bread slice toasted side up on a plate. Top with one lettuce leaf, then the avocado, then the tomato, then the bacon, the other lettuce leaf, and finally the other bread slice, toasted side down. Admire that fine masterpiece. Eat the hell out of it. Don't share. Namaste.

A MOST SUCCESSFUL BLAT

I bet you thought the BLAT would be a simple sandwich to make. Well, if you want to make one that's truly texturally superior, you'll need to follow some extremely rigid advice in regard to each component:

Bread: Using thin, but not *too* thin, bread means you get a good ratio of bread to fillings. Don't burn the bread, because then the texture (not to mention the flavor) gets weird when carbonized toast dust coats your tongue. Don't use hippie bread, because you don't want too much texture here or it will throw off the balance. FYI, any bread with sunflower seeds is considered hippie bread according to the Hippie Bread Institute of Greater Berkeley.

Mayonnaise: Mayo is used for its richness and creaminess but also because mayo makes everything better—unless you hate it and then you're probably not reading this recipe anyway. Feel free to make your own, though honestly Best Foods mayonnaise is just fine.

Avocado: Avocado is used for its creaminess, but make sure you cut the slices thin enough so they lay one over the other nicely. Thicker slices will want to roll and squirt out when you bite down into the sandwich.

Tomato: The texture of the tomato adds a lot to the sandwich, but most significantly it's a source of moisture. The gel in the center of the tomato coats the other ingredients, making the toast seem refreshingly crisp without being dry.

Lettuce: This is not the time or place to get snobby and replace the iceberg lettuce with fancier bibb or green leaf varieties. The lettuce is here purely for its cold, refreshing crunch and to hold the sandwich fillings in place. (I find that positioning it against the bread at top and bottom helps with this.)

Bacon: OK, the bacon is all about the chew and the crunch, so make sure you're not putting flaccid, poorly rendered bacon on this (or any!) sandwich. Cook it correctly (see how in this video: bit.ly/2qGrDA2) and then let it cool off a bit before you build the sandwich. Hot bacon wilts the lettuce and warms the tomato (just no!).

Tomato Salad with Mustard Caviar and Tomato-Cucumber Ice MAKES AS MUCH AS YOU WANT

I make this dish during the final days of summer in Seattle when colorful heirloom tomatoes are perfectly ripe and plentiful (we're talking two to three precious weeks tops). I especially love the textural contrast of the tomatoes against the pop of the pickled mustard seeds and the creamy cold tomato-cucumber ice.

- Variety of heirloom tomatoes and cherry tomatoes, sliced into rounds, wedges, or halved
- Maldon sea salt
- Mustard Caviar (page 161)

- Handful of tiny fresh herb leaves and sprigs, such as basil, dill, or lemon balm
- Favorite extra-virgin olive oil
- Tomato-Cucumber Ice (recipe follows)

1 Just before serving, sprinkle a little bit of salt on each tomato (not too much as the mustard seeds are a bit salty). Spoon little dots of the mustard caviar here and there on the tomatoes, but not too much. Garnish with the herbs, then generously drizzle the olive oil over the top. Scoop a spoonful of the ice into the center of the plate and serve.

Tomato-Cucumber Ice MAKES ABOUT 2 CUPS

- 1 large red tomato, chopped
- 1 small cucumber, peeled and chopped
- 1½ tablespoons seasoned rice wine vinegar
- 1 teaspoon sugar
- ¼ teaspoon fine sea salt

1 Combine the tomato, cucumber, vinegar, sugar, and salt in a blender. Blend well and then pass through a fine-mesh strainer, pressing on the solids with a rubber spatula and discarding anything left behind. Chill the strained mixture well and transfer to an ice cream maker. Process according to the manufacturer's instructions. Transfer the ice to an airtight container and place in the freezer for at least 2 hours. Alternatively, if you don't have an ice cream maker, you can pour the strained mixture into a glass dish, place in the freezer, and stir every 20 minutes until it resembles sorbet.

Chapter Eleven

COLOR, BOOZE, AND EVERYTHING ELSE

Think of the best meal you've ever had. Or not even the best. Think of your last really good meal. I'm going to guess it wasn't all one color, without alcohol in either the food or as an accompaniment (unless you don't drink), served cold when it was supposed to be hot, taking place in a really loud construction zone, and eaten alongside people you don't much like. Salt, acid, sweet, fat, bitter, umami, aromatics, bite, and texture are crucial in getting you to like what is on your plate, but many other factors—some having nothing at all to do with the food or drink directly—equally influence your enjoyment. So much so that I'd be remiss if I didn't cover them.

Color

A famous example of how color can affect our perceptions involved white wine that was dyed red and then given to fifty-four students of oenology (wine science). All of them misidentified the aromas of the wine as belonging to those consistent with red wine. Whoops. Admittedly, it was a tricky setup, but still, one would think a few in the group would say, "Hey, this doesn't smell anything like any red wine I've ever smelled before and it has all the aromas you'd find in white wines."[34] In another study, subjects were served steak, fries, and peas that appeared to be normal in a room where special lights had been installed. When the lighting returned to normal, participants realized that the steak they were eating was (dyed) blue, the fries were (dyed) green, and the peas were (dyed) red. Most lost their appetite completely and some got sick to their stomach, even though the dye was harmless.[35]

Making a dish attractive is the quest of all the world's chefs. But can you break the rules of constructing a colorful plate if everything else is perfectly executed? Yes, you can. Massimo Bottura, Michelin-starred chef of Osteria Francescana in Modena, has a famous dish featuring five ages of Parmigiano-Reggiano. Each age of cheese takes a different form and texture; the plate consists of a foam, cracker, froth, soufflé, and sauce. The color? Shades of white, off-white, and blonde. A chef with lesser skills serving a chicken breast and mashed potatoes with a white sauce? Not very appealing. (That being said, biscuits and gravy are one of the least attractive yet better-tasting dishes around.) Very few people have the skills to do what is essentially a monochromatic dish and still make it spectacular. Bottura does. The texture, flavor, and concept are so well thought out that you completely overlook the anemic color palette—and even better, begin to see subtle color differences between Parmigiano-Reggiano aged for one year versus five. So should you try to bust out an all orange dinner? Well, is your name Massimo Bottura? No? Then probably not.

Booze

Alcohol is volatile (evaporates easily) and when it evaporates up into your nose, flavor compounds from food hitch a ride. Simply stated, booze makes your food smell better. Compare the smell of lemonade to the smell of limoncello. No contest which one has a more powerful, intense lemon aroma. If you want to improve the aromatics of macerating cherries, hit them with a tiny splash of kirsch (cherry brandy)—but not too much or the smell of the alcohol itself will dominate. Likewise, add a spot of limoncello to a lemon tart for some heady next-level cooking.

Alcohol improves flavor by acting as a mediator between fat and water, bonding with both. Fat and water don't bond well with each other, so by inviting booze into this molecular three-way, aromatic compounds (typically fat-soluble) in food (which is mostly water) can cross more easily into the promised land, aka your olfactory cells—command central for the perception of flavor.[36]

Cooking with alcohol absolutely ups the flavor game in your cooking, but only when it makes sense (pro tip: not in guacamole). So pour a little booze into the pot and add it to sauces to dramatically increase the flavor quotient. Do keep in mind that it's a myth that the alcohol burns off completely during cooking. In a flambé (does anyone still flambé?), 75 percent of the alcohol remains; in a braise that's cooked for 2½ hours, 5 percent is retained.[37]

Probably most importantly, alcohol helps you to create memorable meals because of its social lubricant powers, putting people into a relaxed state where the food, the company, everything is a little bit more fun. Fact: your disaster of a dish tastes much better when you're pleasantly buzzed.

Alcohol can also ruin a dinner, either when there isn't any or when there's far too much. If you don't drink, you are probably way more aware of imperfections in the food (and maybe imperfections in your dinner guests), unless of course you like weed—in that case, you *love* the food *soooo* much, it's the best food you've ever had in your *whoooole* life.

My wife, April, is a trained sommelier, so I have an ace in the hole when I need great wine pairings for my private chef dinners. Over the years she's taught me some great tips for pairing food with wine (and cider and beer). Match the body of the food to the body of the wine. A rich, heavy meat dish needs a big (higher in alcohol), bold red wine that helps to cut the fat. Unless it's spicy. Don't pair spicy foods with high alcohol and tannic red wines. The alcohol and tannins aggravate your already aggravated palate, making the chiles seem even hotter. In general, don't pair spicy foods with high acid wines because acid exacerbates the heat, though there are exceptions. Try a jalapeño with a high acid sauvignon blanc and your mouth will catch on fire. High acid, off-dry Rieslings that have residual sugar, however, can still work with spicy dishes because the sugar balances the chiles. Take that same jalapeño pepper with an off-dry Riesling and you will taste the depth of flavor in both the wine and the chile. Light beers are never wrong with spicy food.

Forget that red wine goes with meat and white wine goes with fish—that expression was current when *M*A*S*H* was still on the air. If you don't know what *M*A*S*H* is, then you probably don't know that we ever had segregation in wine and food pairing. Pay closer attention to the body and weight of the dish. A salmon dish with wild mushrooms would be lovely with a pinot noir. A pork tenderloin with apples and fennel would be fantastic paired with a full-bodied white, such as a California chardonnay or Viognier. It's possible to pair food with cocktails, but because most cocktails are high-alcohol concoctions with varying levels of bitterness and sweetness, it takes greater skill to get it right.

Temperature

It's been a long day at work and you reach for a beer and it's lukewarm. Disappointed? Not if you were in a tavern in the nineteenth century. Poor quality could be hidden in warm—even hot—ale concoctions, and even high-quality warm or hot ale was a comforting beverage for people escaping the cold. Bitterness is more apparent at cooler temperatures, so warm ale would decrease the perception. It's hard to imagine anyone these days choosing warm beer, but with all the hopped-up bitter brews that are currently popular, it might not be the worst idea ever. You can test this temperature-bitterness relationship by ordering a drip coffee (Starbucks would be a good choice for its notable dark roast bitterness), letting it cool, and then ordering another hot one. Compare and contrast—you'll likely notice the bitterness more acutely in the tepid version.

Sweetness is magnified at warmer temperatures.[38] I learned this at four years old, when I took a bite of melted ice cream and realized it tasted way sweeter than frozen. From that discovery forward, I'd stir my ice cream around and around my grandma's white china bowl with scalloped edges, *ka-link-ka-lunk-ka-link*, until it became soft-serve, annoying the hell out of my family. This is precisely the reason ice cream bases are oversweetened; most people eat ice cream frozen, the way it was intended to be served. If the base were sweetened for consumption in liquid form, the sweetness would be barely perceptible when frozen.

You too can explore this relationship between temperature and sweetness while justifying eating a lot of ice cream for science. Buy a pint of ice cream, take out one scoop, and let it sit at room temperature until it's completely melted. Taste this first. Record the sweetness level on a scale of 1 to 10 where 1 is sickly sweet and 10 is barely sweet. Rinse your mouth out with water. Take out another scoop and let it soften, stirring it until it has the consistency of soft-serve. Taste this second. Record the sweetness level again. Rinse your mouth out with water. Finally, take a spoonful directly from the carton in the freezer like an animal. Stand there and eat it. Record the sweetness level. Unless you're a quitter, finish the pint.

The moral: always season food at the temperature at which you will be serving it. If you change the serving temperature, taste and reseason or re-balance accordingly.

Sound

〰〰〰〰〰

Bet you didn't think you ate with your ears, but *surprise!* you do, and I've got some science to back this up. In one study, test subjects rated Pringles as "fresher" when they had a crunching sound piped into their ears through headphones.[39] In another study, participants perceived saltiness and sweetness as less intense when they ate the food with loud background noise; conversely, they found the food more intense when they ate it with quieter or no background noise.[40] To put all of this in plain English, it would appear that hearing crispy crunchiness when you're eating something crunchy is a good thing, but eating a nice meal in a really loud restaurant will diminish your experience. This sounds like common sense for the most part and certainly jibes with my personal experience. I really don't mind my wife crunching chips when *I'm* eating chips (but not when I'm not). I tell my students to close their eyes and be quiet when they want to focus on what they are tasting. The flavor comes alive in a way it doesn't when there is loud music and talking.

Matching an appropriate, contextual sound with food can also enhance the eating experience. One of the best oysters I ever ate was standing knee deep in Totten Inlet eating a Virginica oyster while seagulls called over my head and the waves gently lapped at the shoreline. Eating while immersed in the habitat of the ingredient? Priceless and, as it turned out, extra specially delicious.

Charles Spence, head of the Crossmodal Research Laboratory in the Department of Experimental Psychology at Oxford University, would agree. Spence has worked with chef Heston Blumenthal on incorporating sound into a diner's eating experience. Called "Sound of the Sea," Spence and Blumenthal cocreated a dish that was plated on edible "sand" with sea foam and the sound of crashing waves and seagull cries piped into the diner's ears through headphones connected to an iPod hidden in a conch shell. They also had diners listen to the clattering sound of cutlery instead of the sea sounds and not too surprisingly, those who listened to the sound of the sea rated the dish as significantly better tasting.

The Company You Keep

Quick, don't think too hard. You're in a restaurant. What's more important: the quality of the food or the customer service?

I love food and have built my life around it, but I'll be the first to admit it's the customer service and the company I keep

WORDS TO LIVE BY

Michael Pollan has a good rule about food: "Eat food. Not too much. Mostly plants."

Here's my take: Eat mostly whole foods. Don't follow any diets that tell you any foods are bad. Food isn't bad, people are bad. Remember that. Probably don't follow any diets, period. Enjoy your food as you're eating it. Eat it with good, positive people. Unless you're being told not to by a doctor, allow yourself to have any food you want, even if it's a bit of candy or a burger or fried. Drink wine. Cocktails too. Unless you drink them too much, then you should probably cut that shit out. Practice moderation so you can keep eating fat and sugar and booze from time to time. Life is short. Eat mostly whole foods.

when eating that I value above the quality of the food. I literally won't enjoy my food (no matter how great it is) if anyone in my party is treated poorly or treating each other poorly. Bad company or poor service can leave a bad taste in anyone's mouth. I'll give restaurants three chances to get the food right, but I'll never go back if the customer service is horrible. I won't tell you how many chances I give my friends and family.

So take this book with the following grain of salt: if you want to enjoy your food and you want your guests to enjoy the food, share it with as much enthusiasm and happiness as you can muster. Don't apologize if it's not as good as you wanted it to be because it will bias people's enjoyment factor. It's hard not to apologize, I've done it many times, but the manner in which you serve the food, the mood in the room, the quality of conversation—all of these things contribute to how the food tastes

Think right now about a few of the best meals you've ever had. I can guarantee they didn't occur along with bad customer service or with your family while you were in the middle of a fight. Atmosphere is so important to the perception of food enjoyment that I bet some of those "best meals of your life" occurred while you were newly in love, on vacation, or in a foreign country. There's this condition that exists—I've named it Vacation Head—when the food you're eating is the best food that you've ever had in your whole life, in large part because you're on vacation, relaxed and present. Now, I'm not denying that the food is great, but I bet I could make you the same exact meal and serve it to you in your home on a regular weeknight and you would rate it less favorably. It's one of the reasons why all food tastes good when you're camping; even a handful of trail mix out in the woods is arguably better than it would be while sitting in an office.

All of this is to say, pay close attention to all the aspects of taste and flavor I've laid out but not to the exclusion of the company you keep and the environment in which you eat. It all matters.

Chapter Twelve

THE TOTAL DISH

There's a principle in philosophy called Occam's razor, and it essentially means that the simplest explanation is most likely the correct one. We've learned that salt is the most likely problem you will need to solve in your food. I've taught you how to check whether the salt is right on the money. Using Occam's razor, if you are finding that you are not happy with a dish, the most likely explanation is that there isn't enough salt. If you're sure the salt is right, next check the acid, and after that, look to see that sweetness, bitterness, fat, and umami are all in balance. Only then should you move on to aromatics, bite, and texture. Finally look at the elements mentioned in Chapter 11.

When you follow Occam's razor and systematically reach for the most likely fixes first, you will quickly learn to get to a better dish faster. As I've noted several times already, look to classic recipes from the great cuisines of the world for delicious dishes that consider all the elements of taste and flavor I've discussed.

Let's take something as pedestrian sounding as the BLAT sandwich from Chapter 10. You might consider its mother sandwich, the BLT, one of the great sandwiches of American cuisine. I wanted to find a way to quantify why certain dishes hit all the right notes as to be nearly universally beloved within a culture. Here's a hypothetical: there are two food trucks in a parking lot, one is selling BLATs and the other is selling tuna melts. Which one has a line around the block and which one has only a handful of customers? Why would the BLAT have a much larger following? Both sandwiches contain mayonnaise. Both have umami (bacon and tuna and cheese). Both have fat and salt and acidity. What's the difference?

Enter the Flavorator 2000, a mathematical system I created to analyze different dishes and quantify their merits based on

FLAVORATOR
2000

bacon

1 point for each element
salt
aromatics
fat
texture
umami
5
points

all the categories we've discussed. What I hope that it helps to point out is exactly why some dishes are so exciting to your palate and others fall short. The higher the total "score" and the more elements of taste and flavor employed, the more exciting the dish is.

How to Use the Flavorator 2000

The idea is to total up a numerical representation of all the elements that make a dish exceptionally pleasing to the palate; points are awarded for each ingredient that hits the mark. Stick to the nine elements of taste and flavor (salt, acid, sweet, bitter, umami, fat, aromatics, bite, texture); don't assign points for Chapter 11 elements.

Here's how it works in practice: Assign a point when an ingredient is well known to offer a hit of, let's say, umami. The tuna in a tuna melt has umami (being a protein-based food) so it would get 1 point for umami. Mayonnaise has sugar, salt, fat (egg yolk and oil), and acid (lemon) so it earns 1 point for sweet, 1 point for salt, 1 point for fat (don't score fat twice in a sauce like this), and 1 point for acid. Thus mayonnaise scores a 4. The lettuce in a BLAT is iceberg and used for its crunchy texture. Score 1 for texture. Let's say a dish has a bitter ingredient that acts as a balancer for other components, such as the bitters in a Manhattan—it would earn 1 point for bitter. If a dish has numerous spices, assign 1 point for aromatics, not multiple points. Only assign 1 point for salt, even if you sprinkle some on the tomato and some on the avocado. If a fat is used twice in a recipe, it only gets 1 point; however, if a subrecipe uses fat, it gets its own point. Assign 1 bonus point if the dish hits seven or more of the nine elements of taste and flavor.

In my experience, complete dishes that score higher than 10 points (sauce plus what is being sauced, for example, or a sandwich and all of its components) are usually very popular.

Dishes that score over 15 points are addictive, top-level, all-around winners and pretty universally loved within a culture, if not so incredible as to break down cultural barriers. Let's put this into action and compare and contrast the BLAT and the tuna melt and see which one ends up scoring higher.

Texturally Superior BLAT

TASTE	POINTS	INGREDIENTS
SALT	2	bacon, mayonnaise
ACID	2	mayonnaise (lemon), tomato
SWEET	1	mayonnaise (sugar)
FAT	3	bacon, avocado, mayonnaise
BITTER		
UMAMI	2	tomato, bacon
AROMATICS	1	bacon (smoke)
BITE		
TEXTURE	3	bread, lettuce, bacon
BONUS	1	
TOTAL	15	

Tuna Melt

TASTE	POINTS	INGREDIENTS
SALT	2	cheese, mayonnaise
ACID	1	mayonnaise (lemon)
SWEET	1	mayonnaise (sugar)
FAT	2	cheese, mayonnaise
BITTER		
UMAMI	2	cheese, tuna
AROMATICS		
BITE		
TEXTURE	2	bread, celery
BONUS		
TOTAL	10	

BLAT's 15 to tuna's 10. What's the difference? It literally comes down to the bacon. Without bacon, the BLAT, now a LAT, would score a 10.

Now that you know how the Flavorater 2000 works, let's run some of the other recipes from this book through its paces. Compare *nuoc cham*, what I consider one of the most balanced and exciting sauces of Vietnamese cuisine, to ketchup, the ubiquitous sauce of America.

Nuoc Cham

TASTE	POINTS	INGREDIENTS
SALT	1	fish sauce
ACID	1	lime
SWEET	2	sugar, carrot
FAT		

TASTE	POINTS	INGREDIENTS
BITTER		
UMAMI	1	fish sauce
AROMATICS		
BITE	2	garlic, Thai chiles
TEXTURE		
BONUS		
TOTAL	7	

Ketchup

TASTE	POINTS	INGREDIENTS
SALT	1	salt
ACID	2	tomato, vinegar
SWEET	1	brown sugar
FAT	1	oil
BITTER		
UMAMI	1	tomato
AROMATICS		
BITE	1	onion
TEXTURE		
BONUS		
TOTAL	7	

Both sauces score a 7, adding weight to my theory that *nuoc cham* is the "ketchup" of Vietnam.

How about another? I've made my version of Italian salsa verde for the last ten years or so in my classes and for my clients, and I don't think I've ever met someone who didn't fall in love with it. It's addictive and exciting. It's only a sauce and not even a complete dish, yet it already scores over 10 points.

Italian Salsa Verde

TASTE	POINTS	INGREDIENTS
SALT	2	capers, salt
ACID	2	sherry vinegar, capers
SWEET	1	raisins
FAT	2	olive oil, unsalted almonds
BITTER		
UMAMI	1	capers
AROMATICS	2	parsley, unsalted almonds
BITE	1	red pepper flakes
TEXTURE		
BONUS	1	
TOTAL	12	

Almost every element in this book is represented in this dish and I know that's why I keep going back to it year after year and never tire of it. A dish doesn't need to be complicated to hit all the right notes (see the Texturally Superior BLAT recipe on page 182), but it does need to have carefully selected ingredients kept in perfect balance.

Cinnamon and Ginger–Scented Lamb Stew with Tamarind Sauce and Saffron and Turmeric Rice Pilaf MAKES 6 TO 8 SERVINGS

This lamb stew is braised in Indian spices and served with a spicy, bright tamarind sauce and accompanied by a saffron pilaf.

For the lamb stew:

- 2 pounds lamb shoulder, cut into 2-inch cubes
- 2 teaspoons fine sea salt
- 1 tablespoon high-heat oil, such as coconut
- 1 tablespoon cumin seeds
- 1 tablespoon coriander seeds
- 1 teaspoon ground turmeric
- ½ teaspoon cayenne
- 1 cinnamon stick, broken into pieces
- 5 pods green cardamom
- 2 onions, cut into small dice
- ¼ cup julienned ginger
- ½ cup dry white wine or dry white vermouth
- 2 cups unsalted or low-salt beef stock
- 1 (28-ounce) can fire-roasted diced tomatoes
- 1 tart apple, cut into small dice
- ¼ cup raisins
- Zest and juice of 1 lemon
- 1 bay leaf

For the tamarind sauce:

- 2 tablespoons tamarind paste mixed with 2 tablespoons water, or ¼ cup tamarind concentrate
- 1 bunch cilantro (stems OK)
- 1 serrano chile (membranes and seeds removed for less heat)
- 1 teaspoon honey
- ½ teaspoon fine sea salt

- Saffron and Turmeric Rice Pilaf (recipe follows), for serving

1 Salt the lamb at least 2 to 4 hours ahead and refrigerate until you are ready to proceed with cooking.

2 Preheat the oven to 300 degrees F.

3 Heat the coconut oil in an ovenproof braising pot over medium-high heat. Add the lamb and brown well on all sides, leaving behind any fat. Set the meat aside.

4 Meanwhile, combine the cumin, coriander, turmeric, cayenne, cinnamon, and cardamom in a spice grinder until finely ground. Add the spices to the fat in the pot and cook until they start to sizzle and smell, about 30 seconds. Add the onion and ginger and sauté for 5 to 7 minutes, or until the onions are translucent. Deglaze the pot with the wine.

5 Return the lamb to the pot and add the beef stock, tomatoes, apple, raisins, lemon zest (not the juice), and bay. Transfer the pot to the oven and cook, uncovered, for 2 to 3 hours, or until the meat falls apart easily. Season to taste with lemon juice and salt.

6 While the lamb cooks, prepare the tamarind sauce. Combine the tamarind-water mixture (or the concentrate), cilantro, serrano, honey, and salt in a blender and puree until smooth. The sauce will keep in the refrigerator for 1 week.

7 Drizzle the tamarind sauce over the stew at the table. Serve with saffron rice pilaf.

Saffron and Turmeric Rice Pilaf MAKES 6 SERVINGS

- 2 cups basmati rice
- ⅛ teaspoon saffron
- 1 tablespoon hot water
- 5 whole cloves
- 5 cardamom pods
- 1 (2-inch) cinnamon stick, broken into pieces
- ½ teaspoon fine sea salt
- 2 tablespoons coconut oil
- ¼ cup minced shallot
- 1 tablespoon grated fresh turmeric, or 1 teaspoon ground turmeric
- 3 cups unsalted vegetable stock or low-salt vegetable stock
- ¼ cup zante currants or raisins
- 1 teaspoon honey
- ¼ cup pistachios, toasted and chopped

1 Preheat the oven to 350 degrees F.

2 Rinse the rice under cold running water. Drain well. Soften the saffron in the hot water. Combine the cloves, cardamom, cinnamon, and salt in a spice grinder and grind into a fine powder.

3 Heat the coconut oil in an ovenproof sauté pan with lid over medium-high heat. Add the shallot and turmeric and sauté for a few minutes. Add the spice blend and toast for 1 minute. Add the rice and sauté until it dries out and toasts a bit, about

5 minutes. Add the softened saffron with water, vegetable stock, currants, and honey. Stir well and bring to a boil. Cover the pan tightly, transfer to the oven, and bake for 20 minutes.

4 Remove the pan from the oven but keep the lid on for another 10 minutes. Fluff the rice and serve with toasted pistachios on top.

Cinnamon and Ginger–Scented Lamb Stew with Tamarind Sauce and Saffron and Turmeric Rice Pilaf

Lamb Stew

TASTE	POINTS	INGREDIENTS
SALT	1	salt
ACID	4	wine, lemon, tomatoes, tart apple
SWEET	2	raisins, tart apple
FAT	2	coconut oil, lamb
BITTER		
UMAMI	1	lamb
AROMATICS	1	cumin, coriander, turmeric, cinnamon, cardamom, bay
BITE	3	cayenne, onion, ginger
TEXTURE		
BONUS		

Sauce

TASTE	POINTS	INGREDIENTS
SALT	1	salt
ACID	1	tamarind
SWEET	1	honey

TASTE	POINTS	INGREDIENTS
FAT		
BITTER		
UMAMI		
AROMATICS	1	cilantro
BITE	1	serrano
TEXTURE		
BONUS		

Pilaf

TASTE	POINTS	INGREDIENTS
SALT	1	salt
ACID		
SWEET	2	honey, currants
FAT	1	coconut oil
BITTER		
UMAMI		
AROMATICS	1	saffron, cloves, cardamom, cinnamon, turmeric
BITE	1	shallot
TEXTURE	1	pistachios
BONUS		

TOTAL	26 + 1 Bonus = 27

ACKNOWLEDGMENTS

Thanks to all my students at PCC and the Pantry for inspiring me to write this book.

Thank you in no particular order to Linda Hierholzer, Michele Redmond, Chef Stuart Lane and the fantastic staff at Artusi and Spinasse for keeping me well fed and *drunked*, Jerry Traunfeld, Barb Stuckey, Matthew Amster-Burton, Raghavan Iyer, Brad Thomas Parsons, Brandi Henderson, Shirley Corriher, Ashlyn Forshner, Janet Beeby, Greg Atkinson, Karen Jurgensen, Annette Hottenstein, Heather Weiner, Kimberly King Schaub, Anne Livingston, Jill Lightner, Emily Wines, Chris Tanghe, Alicia Guy, Tamara Kaplan, Jacqueline Church, Jami Kimble, Danielle Fague, Claudia Diller, Marc "Poodle" Schermerhorn, the Grialou-Prichards, Kabian and Liz Rendel, CJ Tomlinson, Shannon Kelley, Shannon Romano, Gunilla Eriksson, Robyn Howisey, Colleen Morris, Libby Grant, Irvin Lin, Karyn Schwartz, Christy Wendt Keating, Ian Ireland, Julie Whitehorn, Kim Brauer, Caroline Ferguson, Trevis Gleason, Nadia, Flusche, Andrea Robinson Frabotta, Nancy Leson, Sara Powell Dow Chrisman, Julie Kodama, Jennifer Brault, Melissa Aaron, Debbie Royer, Matthew Johnson, Kirsten Dixon, Sonia Carlson, Mary Pierce, Chris Duvall, Rachel Belle Krampfner, Jameson Fink, Bud Wurtz, Chuck Tessaro, Dave Wei, Deborah Binder, Donna Bell, Erica Finsness, Erik and Mary Josberger, Kathleen Dickenson, Maureen Batali, Nan McKay, Roberta Nelson, Suzannah Kirk-Daligcon, Tamara Barr, and Shirley, Sharon, and Javier at Squirrel Chops for keeping me hyper-caffeinated and agreeing to be my lab rats.

Thanks to my editor Susan Roxborough and publisher Gary Luke for agreeing to publish this book, one of the most difficult and satisfying I've ever written. My thanks to Tony Ong, Anna Goldstein, Em Gale, and the rest of the staff at Sasquatch Books. Thanks also to copyeditor Rachelle Longé McGhee. Thank you to my agent Sharon Bowers for all your support. Finally, to Jeremy Selengut and Jesse Selengut for their helpful comments, Dad and Brenda for inviting me home to write, and April for her enthusiastic cheerleading and unflinching support.

APPENDIX

Recipe Fix Cheat Sheet

Too salty?	Dilute or add bulk. Halve the batch and make a new unsalted batch to stir in. Bump up the sweetness to distract. Add acidity to turn down perception of salt. Add fat to coat the tongue.
Too acidic?	Add sweetness to balance the acid. Add fat to coat the tongue. Dilute or add bulk.
Too sweet?	Balance with acidity. Add something with bite, especially chiles, to distract. Dilute or add bulk. Add fat to coat the tongue.
Too fatty?	Try to defat, if possible. Add acidity to cut the fat. Serve with starch to absorb excess fat.
Too bitter?	Add salt to turn down perception of bitter. Caramelize or add sweetness to balance. Rinse or blanch ingredients, if it makes sense (greens, for example). Dilute or add bulk. Add fat to coat the tongue. Serve the dish hot to turn down perception of bitterness.
Too aromatic?	Dull by adding fat to coat the tongue. Swirl more butter into a pan sauce or hit it with a little cream. Dilute or add bulk. Add a different herb or spice to distract.
Too many chiles? Mouth on fire?	Dairy! Dairy! Dairy! Fat. Add sweetness to distract. Dilute or add bulk. Serve with lots of rice, bread, or another starch.
Too oniony or garlicky?	Keep cooking! Add sweetness or acidity to distract. Dilute or add bulk.

NOTES

1   A 2015 study at Purdue University cited in the journal *Chemical Senses* discovered fat as a recognizable sixth taste easily distinguished by subjects from other basic tastes. They named this taste *oleogustus*. *Oleo* is a Latin root word for oily or fatty and *gustus* refers to taste. Cordelia A. Running, Bruce A. Craig, Richard D. Mattes, "Oleogustus: The Unique Taste of Fat," *Chemical Senses*, 40, no 7 (2015): 507–516, doi: 10.1093/chemse /bjv036.

2   In Ayurvedic medicine six basic tastes are recognized: sweet, sour, salty, bitter, pungent (similar to what I refer to as "piquant," which includes onions, chiles, garlic, cloves, and mustard), and astringent (referring to the tannins present in grape skins and tea, for example). www.chopra.com/articles/the-6-tastes-of -ayurveda#sm.000kabngu12h7ehewtdlxlcq8mw4n.

3   C. Bushdid, M. O. Magnasco, L. B. Vosshall, A. Keller, "Humans Can Discriminate More than 1 Trillion Olfactory Stimuli," *Science*, 343, no 6177 (2014): 1370–2, doi: 10.1126/science.1249168.

4   "How Does Our Sense of Taste Work?" *PubMed Health*, August 17, 2016, https://www.ncbi.nlm.nih.gov/pubmedhealth /PMH0072592/.

5   Jean-Pierre Royet, Jane Plailly, Anne-Lise Saive, Alexandra Veyrac, Chantal Delon-Martin, "The Impact of Expertise in Olfaction," *Frontiers in Psychology*, 4, no 928 (2013), doi: 10.3389 /fpsyg.2013.00928.

6   Not all ethnic groups "taste" food the same way. Among Caucasians in North America, 30 percent are unable to detect the bitterness of PROP, but only 3 percent of Japanese, Chinese, and West Africans were unable to detect the bitterness. Meanwhile nearly 40 percent of Indians were unable to detect the bitterness. Scientists are unsure why there is so much variation between taster groups among these different populations, but what I find fascinating is how this may have affected the cuisine and ingredient or seasoning choices in these various groups. Adam Drewnowskia, Susan Ahlstrom Hendersona, Amy Beth Shorea, Anne Barralt-Fornella, "Nontasters, Tasters and Supertasters of

6-n-Propylthiouracil (PROP) and Hedonic Response to Sweet," *Physiology and Behavior*, 62, no 3 (1997).

7   Sung Kyu Ha, "Dietary Salt Intake and Hypertension," *Electrolyte Blood Press*, 12, no 1 (2014): 7–18, doi: 10.5049/EBP.2014.12.1.7.

8   J. Kenji López-Alt, "The Food Lab: More Tips for Perfect Steaks," *Serious Eats* (blog), March 18, 2011, http://www.seriouseats .com/2011/03/the-food-lab-more-tips-for-perfect-steaks.html.

9   Steven Nordin, Daniel A. Broman, Jonas K. Olofsson, Marianne Wulff, "A Longitudinal Descriptive Study of Self-reported Abnormal Smell and Taste Perception in Pregnant Women," *Chemical Senses*, 29, no 5 (2004): 391–402, doi: 10.1093/chemse /bjh040.

10   Djin Gie Liem, Julie A. Mennella, "Heightened Sour Preferences During Childhood," *Chemical Senses*, 28, no 2 (2003): 173–180, doi: 10.1093/chemse/28.2.173.

11   Holly Strawbridge, "Artificial Sweeteners: Sugar-Free, But At What Cost?" *Harvard Health Blog* (blog), July 16, 2012, www .health.harvard.edu/blogartificial-sweeteners-sugar-free-but-at -what-cost-201207165030.

12   Feris Jabr, "How Sugar and Fat Trick the Brain into Wanting More Food," *Scientific American*, January, 1, 2016, http://www .scientificamerican.com/article/how-sugar-and-fat-trick -the-brain-into-wanting-more-food/.

13   Barbara Moran, "Is Butter Really Back? Clarifying the Facts on Fat," *Harvard Public Health*, Fall 2014, www.hsph.harvard.edu /magazine/magazine_article/is-butter-really-back.

14   Dan Buettner, "The Island Where People Forget to Die," *The New York Times Magazine*, October 24, 2012, www.nytimes .com/2012/10/28/magazine/the-island-where-people-forget-to -die.html.

15   Cordelia A Running, Bruce A. Craig, Richard D. Mattes, "Oleogustus: The Unique Taste of Fat," *Chemical Senses*, 40, no 7 (2015): 507–516, doi: 10.1093/chemse/bjv036.

16   Daniel Gritzer, "Cooking With Olive Oil: Should You Fry and Sear in It or Not?" *Serious Eats* (blog), March 24, 2015, www .seriouseats.com/2015/03/cooking-with-olive-oil-faq-safety -flavor.html.

17   J. Kanner, "Dietary Advanced Lipid Oxidation Endproducts Are

Risk Factors to Human Health," *Molecular Nutrition and Food Research* 51, no 9 (2007): 1094–1101.

18   "Sour-Bitter Confusion," *Society of Sensory Professionals*, www
.sensorysociety.org/knowledge/sspwiki/Pages/Sour-Bitter%20
Confusion.aspx.

19   "Why Does Toothpaste Make Things Like Orange Juice Taste So
Awful?" Today I Found Out, January 5, 2017, www.youtube.com
/watch?v=ETnhft-w51Q.

20   Dan Souza, "Why Nacho Cheese Doritos Taste Like Heaven,"
Serious Eats (blog), June 12, 2012, www.seriouseats.com/2012/06
/science-of-chips-ingredients-msg-why-nacho-cheese-doritos
-taste-like-heaven.html.

21   K. Roininen, L. Lahteenmaki, H. Tuorila, "Effect of Umami Taste
on Pleasantness of Low-Salt Soups During Repeated Testing,"
Physiology and Behavior, 60, no 3 (1996): 953–958.

22   Una Masic, Martin R. Yeomans, "Umami Flavor Enhances
Appetite but also Increases Satiety," *The American Journal of
Clinical Nutrition*, 100, no 2 (2014): 532–538, doi: 10.3945
/ajcn.113.080929.

23   Katharine M. Woessner, Ronald A. Simon, Donald D. Stevenson,
"Monosodium Glutamate Sensitivity in Asthma," *The Journal
of Allergy and Clinical Immunology*, 104, no 2 (1999): 305–310, doi:
http://dx.doi.org/10.1016/S0091-6749(99)70371-4.

24   M. Freeman, "Reconsidering the Effects of Monosodium
Glutamate: A Literature Review," *Journal of the American
Academy of Nurse Practitioners*, 18, (2006): 482–486, doi:
10.1111/j.1745-7599.2006.00160.x.

25   Nicholas Eriksson, Shirley Wu, Chuong B. Do, Amy K. Kiefer,
Joyce Y. Tung, Joanna L. Mountain, David A. Hinds, Uta
Francke, "A Genetic Variant Near Olfactory Receptor Genes
Influences Cilantro Preference," *Flavour*, 1, no 1 (2012), doi:
10.1186/2044-7248-1-22.

26   J. Kenji López-Alt, "Freeze Fresh Herbs for Long-Term Storage,"
Serious Eats (blog), March 30, 2015, www.seriouseats
.com/2015/03/how-to-freeze-herbs-for-long-term-storage.html.

27   Gardiner Harris, "F.D.A. Finds 12% of U.S. Spice Imports

Contaminated," *The New York Times*, October 30, 2013, www
.nytimes.com/2013/10/31/health/12-percent-of-us-spice
-imports-contaminated-fda-finds.html.

28   Natalie Wolchover, "Myth Debunked: Spicy Food Doesn't Really
     Kill Taste Buds," Live Science, September 12, 2012, www
     .livescience.com/34213-spicy-food-taste-buds-myth.html.

29   Rita Mirondo, Sheryl Barringer, "Deodorization of Garlic Breath
     by Foods, and the Role of Polyphenol Oxidase and Phenolic
     Compounds," *Journal of Food Science*, 81, no 10 (2016): C2425–
     C2430, doi: 10.1111/1750-3841.13439.

30   Daniel Gritzer, "The Best Way to Mince Garlic," *Serious Eats*
     (blog), January 9, 2015, www.seriouseats.com/2015/01/how
     -to-mince-chop-garlic-microplane-vs-garlic-press.html.

31   "Food Bacteria-Spice Survey Shows Why Some Cultures Like It
     Hot," Cornell Chronicle, (1998): www.news.cornell.edu
     /stories/1998/03/food-bacteria-spice-survey-shows
     -why-some-cultures-it-hot.

32   Duangjai Lexomboon, Mats Trulsson, Inger Wårdh, Marti
     G. Parker, "Chewing Ability and Tooth Loss: Association
     with Cognitive Impairment in an Elderly Population
     Study," *Journal of the American Geriatrics Society*, (2012): doi:
     10.1111/j.1532-5415.2012.04154.x.

33   Helen Coulthard, Gillian Harris, Pauline Emmett, "Delayed
     Introduction of Lumpy Foods to Children During the
     Complementary Feeding Period Affects Child's Food Acceptance
     and Feeding at 7 Years of Age," *Maternal & Child Nutrition*, 5, no 1
     (2008): 75–85, doi: 10.1111/j.1740-8709.2008.00153.x.

34   Gil Morrot, Frederic Brochet, Denis Dubourdieu, "The Color of
     Odors," *Brain and Language*, 79, no 2 (2001): 309-320, doi: 10.1006
     /brln.2001.2493.

35   Eds. H. L. Meiselman and H. J. H. MacFie, *Food Choice Acceptance
     and Consumption*, London, Blackie Academic and Professional,
     1996.

36   David Joachim, Andrew Schloss, "Alcohol's Role in Cooking,"
     Fine Cooking, no 104 (2010): 28–29, www.finecooking.com
     /item/13810/alcohols-role-in-cooking.

37   "USDA Table of Nutrient Retention Factors," U.S. Department of

Agriculture, December 2007, www.ars.usda.gov
/ARSUserFiles/80400525/Data/retn/retn06.pdf.

38   Amalia Mirta Calvino, "Perception of Sweetness: The Effects of
Concentration and Temperature," *Physiology & Behavior*, 36, no 6
(1986): 1021-1028, doi: 10.1016/0031-9384(86)90474-9.

39   M. Zampini, C. Spence, "The Role of Auditory Cues in
Modulating the Perceived Crispness and Staleness of Potato
Chips," *Journal of Sensory Studies*, 19, (2004): 347–363, doi:
10.1111/j.1745-.

40   A. T. Woods, E. Poliakoff, D. M. Lloyd, J. Kuenzel, R. Hodson,
H. Gonda, J. Batchelor, G. B. Dijksterhuis, A. Thomas, "Effect
of Background Noise on Food Perception," *Food Quality and
Preference*, 22, no 1 (2011): 42-47, doi: 10.1016
/j.foodqual.2010.07.003.

BIBLIOGRAPHY

McGee, Harold. *On Food and Cooking*. New York, NY: Scribner, 2004.

McLagan, Jennifer. *Bitter: A Taste of the World's Most Dangerous Flavor, with Recipes*. Berkeley, CA: Ten Speed Press, 2014.

McQuaid, John. *Tasty: The Art and Science of What We Eat*. New York, NY: Scribner, 2015.

Moss, Michael. *Salt Sugar Fat: How the Food Giants Hooked Us*. New York, NY: Random House, 2013.

Mouritsen, Ole G., and Klavs Styrbæk. *Umami: Unlocking the Secrets of the Fifth Taste*. New York, NY: Columbia University Press, 2015.

Prescott, John. *Taste Matters: Why We Like the Foods We Do*. London, UK: Reaktion Books, 2012.

Rodgers, Judy. *The Zuni Cafe Cookbook*. New York, NY: W. W. Norton and Company, 2002.

Stuckey, Barb. *Taste What You're Missing: The Passionate Eater's Guide to Why Good Food Tastes Good*. New York, NY: Simon & Schuster, 2012.

RESOURCES

Where to Buy a PROP Test
http://sensonics.com/taste-products/prop-strips-2.html

Must-Read Books on Taste and Flavor
All the books listed in the Bibliography (see opposite page)
The Food Lab by J. Kenji López-Alt
Salt, Fat, Acid, Heat by Samin Nosrat
Flavor Bible by Andrew Dornenburg and Karen A. Page
The Flavor Thesaurus by Niki Segnit

Must-Read Books on Food Science (Including Baking)
CookWise by Shirley O. Corriher
Modernist Cuisine by Nathan Myhrvold, Chris Young, and
    Maxime Bilet
The Baking Bible by Ruth Levy Beranbaum
The Science of Good Cooking by the editors of America's Test
    Kitchen and Guy Crosby
Cooking for Geeks by Jeff Potter
How to Read a French Fry by Russ Parsons

Must-Visit Websites
SeriousEats.com
CooksScience.com

Must-Read Magazines
Cook's Illustrated

Must-Watch Programs
The Mind of a Chef
Chef's Table

INDEX

A

acidity, 6–7, 13, 16–17, 21, 37–48, 53, 74, 75, 156
  balancing a dish with, 39–41, 52, 60–61
  basics of, 38
  detecting need for, xiv, 39
  recipes, 45–48
  sources of, 40–41, 54
  taste experiment, 44–46
  too much, fixes for, 42, 210
  vinaigrettes, ratio in, 44
acoustic tribology, 68
alcohol, 84, 89, 126, 145, 156, 188–190
  See also wine
aperitifs, 84
aroma, linked to taste, 4–6
aromatics, 13, 75, 111–135
  for adding sweetness without sugar, 56, 63
  basics of, 111–112
  categorizing, by "tone," 112–114, 131
  combining flavors, 130
  extracting flavor from, 74, 126–127, 188–189
  in low-sodium diets, 24–25
  overuse of, fixes for, 127, 210
  recipes, 29–31, 133–135
  scaling up, 115, 128–129
  smoke, 129
  taste experiments, 131–132
  See also citrus zest; garlic; herbs; onions; spices; specific ingredient
artificial sweeteners, 53
astringency, 83, 85

B

baked goods, 17, 58–60, 70
Bartoshuk, Linda, 8, 9
basil, 116
bay leaf, 125
bite, 61, 62, 128, 137–169, 189–190

balancing, in a dish, 139
  effects from eating ingredients with, 137–138
  recipes, 161, 165, 167–169
  taste experiment, 165–166
  See also chiles; garlic; ginger; onions; specific ingredient
bitterness, 6–7, 8, 16–17, 24–25, 51, 83–92, 190
  basics of, 85–86
  recipes, 89, 90–92
  reducing, methods of, 19, 52, 86–87, 88, 210
  taste experiments, 63, 88–89
BLAT, Texturally Superior, 182–183, 197, 200–202
Blumenthal, Heston, 99, 192
booze. See alcohol
Bosland, Paul, 148
Bottura, Massimo, 188
Brauer, Kim, 40
Brisket, Gummy's, 78–80

C

capsaicin, 137, 138, 139–140, 144–147, 172
caramelization, 13, 57, 59, 60, 86
cardamom, 121
Carrot Salad, Spiced, 29–31
chemesthesis, 138
chewing, 172
Chicken Wings, Fiery Roasted Thai Chile, 167–168
children, 38, 83–84, 176
chile oil, 48
chiles, 137, 138, 139–149, 156
  easing pain from, 146–147
  fresh versus dried, 141–142
  heat and flavor categories, 139–141
  heat reduction methods, 143–145, 165–166, 210
  myths about, 148

recipes, 91–92, 105, 165, 167–169
scaling up, 128, 147
substitution ratios for whole and
ground, 143
taste experiment, 165–166
wine, pairing with, 189–190
Chinese cuisine, 164, 174–175
Church, Jacqueline, 163, 164
cilantro, 114, 115–116, 118
citrus zest, 41, 129–130
Coffee and Chocolate–Braised
Short Ribs, 91–92
coffee experiments, 63, 88–89
Coke, 53
color, 187–188
company, 192–194
confit, 75
cookbooks, 13
Cookies, Cacao Nib and Chocolate
Chunk, 65
Cree, Dana, 129

D
Daikon radishes, 159, 161
Dashi, 98, 108
desserts, 19, 39, 58
digestifs, 84
Doering, Richard, 181
Doritos, 96, 97
Dunlop, Fuchsia, 174

E
eggs, 18
experiments. *See* taste experiments

F
Falkowitz, Max, 17
fat, 16–17, 21, 42, 61, 67–80, 87
alcohol and, 177, 188–189
aromatics and, 74, 75, 126, 127
basics of, 68–70
cooking garlic with, 150, 152, 156
detecting need for, 74
excessive, remedies for, 39,
74–75, 210

rancidity, 72–73
recipes, 76–80
reducing spiciness with,
144–145, 156
smoke point, 71–72
substituting types, 71
types of, 70
vinaigrettes, ratio in, 44
fish sauce, 101, 103, 104–106
flavorants, 16, 51
Flavorator 2000, 197–208
Flavor Bible, The (Page and
Dornenburg), 130
flavor-tripping, 39–40
flavor *versus* taste, 3–6
food, rules about, 193
food allergies, 156–157
FoodPairing.com, 130

G
garlic, 111–112, 149–153, 155–157, 161
taste experiment, 165–166
too much, fixes for, 155–156, 210
types of, 152–153
ginger, 137, 157, 158, 161, 205–208
Green, Barry, 138
Gritzer, Daniel, 72, 150–151
guacamole, 22, 113

H
Hänig, David P., 7
Henderson, Brandi, 169
herbs, 13, 74, 84, 112, 114–119
freezing, 118–119
fresh *versus* dried, 114–117
pastes, 119
replacing, 125–126
scaling up, 115, 128–129
substitutions for, 123–125
See also aromatics
horseradish, 137, 158–159, 160
Horseradish Cream, 78–79
hot foods. *See* bite
Hot Sauce, The Pantry's Southern-
Style, 169

I

Ikeda, Kikunae, 98
Iyer, Raghavan, 128, 149

J

Jacobsen, Rowan, 96
jalapeños, 140–141, 147, 189–190
Jam, Honey, Rhubarb, and Thyme, 64
Japanese cuisine, 98, 99, 108, 164, 174, 175
Japanese mint, 124
Jurgensen, Karen, 147

K

kombu, 98, 108
Kuninaka, Akira, 98

L

Lamb Stew with Tamarind Sauce and Saffron and Turmeric Rice Pilaf, Cinnamon and Ginger–Scented, 205–208
Lamb with Coconut Milk Sauce, Sri Lankan Spiced Rack of, 133–134
leftovers, 12, 130–131
lemongrass, 41, 105–106
lemon juice. *See* acidity
Leson, Nancy, 141
lime leaf, 41, 105–106, 114, 123–124
López-Alt, J. Kenji, 118, 122

M

Maillard reaction, 57
Mangoes, Pickled, 135
Manhattan, Classic, 89
Matzo Ball Soup, Ode to Gummy's, 25–27, 32–35
McGee, Harold, 57, 117
meats, 18, 39, 75, 189, 190
miracle berry, 39–40
Moran, Barbara, 67
Moss, Michael, 16
mouthfeel, 39, 68, 69, 100, 174–175

MSG (monosodium glutamate), 98, 102, 103–104
mushrooms, 101, 108, 178
mustard, 137, 158
  greens, 160, 161
  seeds, 122, 160–161
Mustard Caviar, 161

N

Nuoc Cham, 165
  heat in, 145
  taste score for, 202–203

O

oil. *See* fat
okonomiyaki (savory pancakes), 99
olestra, 71
On Food and Cooking (McGee), 117
onions, 13, 17, 111–112, 149, 153–156, 161, 210

P

Pantry's Southern-Style Hot Sauce, The, 169
paprika, smoked, 124, 129
Parmigiano-Reggiano, 101, 176, 188
parsley, 116, 118, 119
Pasta alla Speranza, 107
peppercorns, 128, 137, 138, 156, 162–164
peppers. *See* chiles
pesto, 118
Pickled Mangoes, 135
Polenta, Creamy, 92
Pollan, Michael, 193
processed foods, 16–17, 40, 67, 96, 97
PROP test strips, 2, 8

R

Radicchio Salad with White Beans and Smoked Sea Salt, Warm, 90
radishes, 158, 159, 161
Ramirez, Marc, 141
rancidity, 72–73
recipe fix cheat sheet, 210

Robinson, Jancis, 163
Rodgers, Judy, 18

S

saffron, 112, 114
Saffron and Turmeric Rice Pilaf, 206–208
Salmon with Miso Vinaigrette and Sesame-Roasted Vegetables, 47–48
salsa verde, freezing, 118
Salsa Verde, Italian, 45–46, 204
salt, 6–7, 11, 13, 15–35, 39, 61, 87, 129, 191, 197
    for bitterness reduction, 19, 88
    detecting need for, xiv, 20–21
    as flavor "conductor," 16–19
    for increasing sweetness, 19, 56, 63, 88
    low-sodium diets, 24–25, 100
    pairing dips and chips, 22
    pepper, separating from, 164
    recipes, 29–35
    scaling up, 128
    taste experiments, 28–31
    too much, fixes for, 21, 52, 210
    types of, 23–24
Salt Sugar Fat (Moss), 16
savoriness. *See* umami
Schwartz, Karyn, 146–147
Scoville Scale, 139–140
"seasoning to taste," xiii
Sethi, Tanmeet, 61, 135
shiitake, dried, 98, 101, 108
shiso leaf, 124
Short Ribs, Coffee and Chocolate–Braised, 91–92
smell, linked to taste, 4–6
smoke, 129
smoked paprika, 124, 129
smoke point, 71–72
sound, 191–192
Soup, Matzo Ball, 32–35
soup, salt in, 17–18, 25–27

Soup, Sweet Potato, with Chile and Lemongrass, 105
sourness, 6–7, 38, 83, 85
    See also acidity
Spence, Charles, 192
Speranza, John, 107
Spiced Carrot Salad, 29–31
spices, 13, 84, 112, 119–127, 131–132
    adding, tips for, 122
    buying, 123, 125–126
    grinding, 121, 127
    scaling up, 128–129
    storing, 123
    substitutions for, 123–125
    toasting, 121–122, 132
    whole *versus* preground, 120
    See also aromatics
spiciness. *See* bite
stock, 26, 74, 119
    Dashi, 108
    Roasted Chicken Stock, 34–35
Stuckey, Barb, 88–89
sumac, 122
super/sensitive tasters, 1–2, 8–10, 87, 138
sweetness, 6–7, 16–17, 21, 42, 51–65, 86, 87, 172
    addiction to, 61–62
    baked goods and, 58–60
    basics of, 51–52
    desserts, 19, 39, 58
    foods benefiting from, 52
    increasing, without sugar, 19, 56, 63, 88
    pairing with spicy foods, 62, 145, 156, 165–166, 189–190
    recipes, 64–65
    substituting sugar types, 53–55, 60
    taste experiment, 63
    temperature and, 53, 190–191
    too much, fixes for, 39, 60–61, 210
    types of, 54–55
Sweet Potato Soup with Chile and Lemongrass, 105

T

Tanghe, Chris, 62, 177–178
tannins, 83, 176–178
taste, as subjective, 12–13
taste experiments, 28–31, 44–46, 63, 88–89, 104–106, 131–132, 165–166, 180–181
taste receptors, 4, 6–7, 20, 85, 98
tasters, super/sensitive, 1–2, 8–10, 87, 138
taste scoring system, 197–208
taste sensitivity, tests for, 8–10
taste *versus* flavor, 3–6
tasting tips, 11–12
tea, lapsang souchong, 129
temperature, 53, 87, 190–191
texture, 59, 68, 69, 75, 100, 171–185, 191–192
    for added interest, 175, 179–180
    appreciation of, 174–175, 178–179
    basics of, 172–173
    as contextual, 176
    recipes, 182–185
    tannins and, 176–178
    taste experiments, 180–181
    types of, 179–180
tomatoes, 38, 99, 101, 113
Tomato Salad with Mustard Caviar and Tomato-Cucumber Ice, 184–185
tongue. *See* taste receptors
toothpaste, 86
Traunfeld, Jerry, 117
trigeminal nerve, 83, 137–138, 172
Turmeric and Saffron Rice Pilaf, 206–208

U

umami, 13, 17, 39, 95–108
    basics of, 95–97
    detecting need for, 100
    discovery of, 98
    food sources, 97, 98–99, 101–102
    recipes, 99, 105–108
    taste experiments, 104–106

V

vegetables, 18, 56, 57, 86–87
Vegetables, Sesame-Roasted, and Salmon with Miso Vinaigrette, 47–48
Vegetables with Dates and Prosciutto Vinaigrette, Roasted Winter, 76–77
videos, 13, 18, 32, 48, 117, 142, 155, 178, 181, 183
Vinaigrette, Miso, 47–48
Vinaigrette, Prosciutto, 76–77
vinaigrettes, fat to acid ratio in, 44
vinegar. *See* acidity

W

wasabi, 137, 158–159, 160, 161
wine, 2, 62, 163, 177–178, 189–190
Wines, Emily, 62

Z

zest, citrus, 41, 129–130